P9-BYA-647

What is Anglicanism?

9 -9 o

by
Urban T. Holmes III

MOREHOUSE PUBLISHING
Harrisburg, PA • Wilton, CT

For Gale D. Webbe

In Gratitude

"Something far greater than Jonah is There" by Robert M. Cooper is quoted with permission from *The Anglican Theological Review,* LVI, 4 (October, 1974), 440-441.

Fifth Printing

Morehouse Publishing
P.O. Box 1321
Harrisburg, Pennsylvania 17105

ISBN 0-8192-1295-4

Library of Congress Catalog Card Number 81-84715

Printed in the United States of America

Table of Contents

Foreword   v

Preface   vii

The Anglican Consciousness   1

Authority in the Church   9

The Bible   17

The Incarnation   25

Church and Sacraments   33

The Liturgy   41

The Episcopacy   49

Pastoral Care   57

Spirituality   65

Mission   73

Church and State   81

Prophetic Witness   89

Foreword

During the last year of his life, Dean Urban T. Holmes, III devoted a major portion of his time, including a sabbatical leave, to writing this book. The subject was of utmost interest and concern to him and in numerous conversations between us as author and editor, his clear convictions and steadfast principles were carefully enunciated. The results of that reflection are presented in this his last book completed approximately three months before his untimely death on August 6, 1981. Had he lived we had plans well under way for successive volumes that would have examined anew the scope of Anglican theology and the broad historical traditions of doctrinal development.

The Episcopal Church, Anglicanism, and the "Via Media" were ever close to Terry Holmes' care and concern as a person, a priest and an educator. It is important to remember his distress with some current trends and developments in the church. Terry Holmes was particularly concerned with and acutely aware of those trends that were oblivious to the rich and inviolate historical traditions of the church. With a clear eye and a sharply developed mind he was impatient with such careless ways and sought to recall the church and its leadership to the great truths of its heritage. In this book that heritage is clearly depicted and then directly related to contemporary life. All of us shall be enriched by this his last endeavor even as we are impoverished without his presence among us.

The proofing for this book was handled by Dean Holmes' daughter, Jane Teresa Holmes. No changes have been made in the text as completed but not revised.

Theodore A. McConnell
Editorial Director
Morehouse-Barlow Co.

Preface

This book is a response to a suggestion made by a friend, who read a report of an interview with me in the Professional Supplement of the October 1980, issue of *The Episcopalian.* In that interview, I had expressed the opinion that many Episcopalians seem to be speaking these days to important matters with little knowledge of our Anglican heritage. His point was that one reason for this is that there is next to no material available to help people know that heritage. He went on to advise that I might try to do something about that lack.

His suggestion fell on fertile ground. In my own evolving life in the church a renewed concern for our Anglican outlook has been awakened. I am convinced that most of us, if not all, are members of this communion for important reasons that we hold dear, but often find difficult to express. A symptom of this is the resistance of many of us to an unthinking appropriation of other styles of belief and practice, which resistance may appear to others as a mere perverse obstinacy. What may be happening is that we cannot verbalize a threatened loss to what we sense very deeply as intrinsic to our Anglican way.

In pursuing this line of thought I have written a book which is necessarily personal. It describes frankly my understanding of what it means to be an Anglican. I can claim for that fifty-one years of active and thoughtful participation in the Episcopal Church, but certainly not an absence of a bias. I have never known two Episcopalians to agree totally, and the fact that we can admit our disagreements is only indicative of our Anglican freedom to acknowledge the polymorphous nature of all human knowing, something not every Christian body is comfortable admitting.

I would argue that my approach is reasonable. I am not saying that it is always analytical or that I have sought to prove my position. This is not what I think Anglicanism intends by being reasonable. By "reasonable" I mean that the argument does not violate in any obvious way a reflective, balanced examination of experience by one who believes himself in love with God.

I am aware that not everyone likes the name for our communion of "Anglican," and may find the title and subsequent discussion irritating. There are those who have taken the title Anglican unto themselves to name their own schismatic groups. Obviously, this is not a practice that can be supported. Occasionally someone comes up with the notion that "Anglican" is the equivalent of "high church," which is wrong. There are others within the Episcopal Church who believe that because Anglican means "English" that it is too provincial. On the contrary, let us acknowledge that the roots of our peculiar way of looking at the Christian experience are provincial; they evolved from the English province of Christendom. This should bother us no more than Roman does the Roman Catholic Church. I mean by Anglican, to be specific, nothing more than those Christians who worship according to some authorized edition of the *Book of Common Prayer* and who are in communion with the see of Canterbury.

In this spirit, I find it much easier to identify Anglicanism with persons rather than a system, although I do not agree that we lack a system. This personal approach has dictated the design of the study, inasmuch as each chapter draws upon some one individual whom I judge to epitomize the point to be made. This will, it is hoped, make the subject matter concrete and more readily appropriated. We are a people-oriented church and it is important that we make a concerted effort to know and celebrate our heroes.

There is no intention to pursue the many obvious loose ends that each chapter leaves dangling. This book is intended to make a beginning for whoever reads it — priest or lay person, inquirer or lifelong member — and to invite an intelligent and ever more informed quest. I am of the opinion that it is neither possible nor desirable to make a neat package, but there is spiritual growth in the effort.

Sometimes the only thing outsiders recall about the Episcopal Church or Anglicanism is that it is supposedly divided into high church and low church. Inasmuch as this is a gross simplification of a very complicated history of Anglicanism and is fundamentally untrue, there is no discussion of that issue in this book. I have sought to take a position which I believe to be consistent with the theology of the 1979 *Book of Common Prayer* of the Episcopal Church. This book promises among those who listen to lay to rest the so-called churchmanship controversies that have sapped the energy of the Anglican Church for far too long.

Some years ago I had the occasion to preach in a seminary chapel on the Feast of the Bestowal of the American Episcopate (November 14). It provided an occasion for a "cradle Episcopalian" such as myself to ask why he was an Anglican. The answer that came to me then and remains with me is that, with all its irritating nonsense, I know of no place in which I could have more freedom to be that Catholic Christian which we are called to be. I leave it for the reader to ponder my meaning.

On how many occasions have I delighted in expressing thanks to those who made a book possible. The list always differs a bit. This time there is the University of the South and Robert Ayres, its Vice-Chancellor, who acknowledged my need for a sabbatical leave. Robert Haden, LaRue Downing and Ed Hartley all gave me a place to work and time to do it at the Kanuga Conference Center in Hendersonville, North Carolina. I am grateful to Lisa Kirby, who typed the manuscript. The Rector, Alex Viola, and the people of St. James Church, Hendersonville, warmly welcomed my wife and me to their lively community, and as a result, I found new enthusiasm to write thankfully of our Anglican heritage.

The book is dedicated to one who lives in Hendersonville, a quiet, deeply devoted priest, who has been my mentor and friend for more than thirty-eight years. As one grows older he realizes who counts to him, and Gale Webbe is one right at the top of my list.

Urban T. Holmes
Monday in Holy Week, 1981

Chapter One

The Anglican Consciousness

Anglicanism is a mode of making sense of the experience of God. To put it another way, Anglicanism is a particular approach to the construction of reality, or to the building of a world.

What do I mean by "building a world"? The point is crucial for our discussion; so this illustration may help. Three couples are planning to take a vacation together and they are discussing whether or not to go to the beach. One couple strongly urges that they go. Think of the sun, the sound of the ocean, they say, lying on the beach with nothing to do but relax. They recall their own youth when trips to the beach were the happiest occasions of their lives. Another couple resists. One of them recalls when as a small child she almost drowned in the ocean. She retains a deep fear of water. The husband finds lying on the beach a waste of time. He recalls a life of having to prove himself by hard work. The third couple is willing to go, but memories of sunburn and a week of rain two years before dampens their enthusiasm.

What is the question here? It is not what is intrinsically the nature of an experience of the beach — "the beach in the raw." None of us ever experience the beach that way. It is what each couple makes of the experience of the beach based upon their memory and its way of shaping their consciousness of the beach that makes the difference. It is not necessarily a matter of whether one couple is right and the rest are wrong, although it would be if one insisted the beach was inhabited by man-eating tigers. Each

1

couple has a distinctive way of building a world of meaning or constructing a reality around the experience of the beach. That world of meaning obviously determines each couple's willingness to go to the beach.

One way of understanding Anglicanism is to know that it is a unique way of looking, making sense, and acting in the experience of God disclosed to us in the person of Jesus Christ. This is to say that it is a manner of being conscious, which manner was given birth in the history of a people whose culture, language and institutions came into being in the British Isles. It is well to remember that these islands, until the discovery and colonization of the New World by Europeans, were the frontier of the civilized world, removed from the centers of culture. It was the end point of successive invasions from the north and east: the Celts, the Anglo-Saxons, the Norse and the Normans (who were Norse that had originally settled in France). Anglican consciousness is the product of a montage of geographical, social, political, economic and racial forces that have created a peculiar historical memory. That memory has been handed on through the centuries, and while modified by subsequent events (e.g., the colonization of North America) remains distinctive at heart.

An example of Anglican consciousness is Julian of Norwich, an obscure fourteenth century anchorite. In some ways Julian was a commonplace phenomenon of her age. She lived in a cell attached to the parish church in an East Anglia town. From a window in her cell she could view the Eucharist and from another window she could assist people seeking spiritual counsel. There were many such persons in later medieval England, but none known to us of the genius of Julian.

In 1370, Julian received a series of revelations or showings, in which the crucified Lord appeared to her. The image of the suffering Christ, which was the persistent form of these visions, was not remarkable for the times. It was consistent with the popular religious art of the century. What is arresting is Julian's reflections upon this experience setting forth the world she constructed out of her experience.

Julian lived in a time of suffering and confusion. The Black Death had wiped out perhaps as much as a third of the population of England. The once proud and noble warrior-king, Edward III, was living out his last years in senility, mourning the death of his promising son, the Black Prince. Edward III was followed by his grandson, Richard II, who was broken against the misfortunes of his times despite his efforts to resolve England's problems. Deposed, Richard II died in prison. Throughout this period England was enduring an incredibly cruel and draining war with France, which we know as the Hundred Years War.

It is in this world that Julian spoke with a certain calm. "Our life is founded," she said, "on faith with hope and love." The basis of her faith was the Christ, who described himself to her as "the ground of her beseeching." Julian was no foolish optimist. She had a deep awareness of our sin, yet believed that God has allowed us to fall that he might raise us up that much higher. "Sin is necessary," she says; but immediately adds in her best known words, "All will be well, and every kind of thing will be well."

What kind of world does Julian see which allows her such confidence in a time of confusion and despair? It begins, first, with sensibility. I use the word "sensibility" in an unfamiliar meaning. It is the ability to apprehend or incorporate into our awareness the totality of an experience in all depth and breadth. Sensibility refers to the capacity to be sensitive and to accept what our senses tell us, even when that is not what fits into our neat categories. It implies an openness to experience, even when the meaning of that experience is ambiguous, incongruous and obscure.

Julian's sensibility is seen in her insistence that God lets us rebel against him in order that he might raise us up even higher, which is a profound paradox. She said that there are five activities that arise in her at the same time: rejoicing, mourning, desire, fear and true hope, meaning that we know Jesus in both consolation and desolation. We are repelled by God and drawn to him at the same moment. There is an ambiguity to our awareness that reflects a consciousness of the experience that is not neatly drawn. Life is like that when perceived in its fullness, light and darkness, with shades of gray in between.

Secondly, Julian is aware that the extraordinary love of God is to be found within the ordinary. The vision of a hazelnut comes to mind, from which Julian learns three things: that God made, loves and preserves his creation. What could be more ordinary than a little hazelnut? Julian had a gift for perceiving what another Englishman, Gerard Manley Hopkins (1844-1889) called the inscape or inner reality of things. This takes a way of seeing beyond the common sense reductions of the cynic, who can only see the outer appearance.

This gift for the extraordinary sometimes works in another direction. The commonplace ideas of the culture can be elevated to illumine the meaning of God in a new way. Julian takes the dying ideal of feudal chivalry, with its notion of the courteous knight, and applies it to God. "For God sees one way and man sees another way," said Julian. "For it is for man to meekly accuse himself, and it is for our Lord God's own goodness courteously to excuse man." The word "courteous" carries all the meaning of mercy, gentleness and compassion. God is seen in a startling new, but recognizable light. He becomes almost human in his goodness.

Thirdly, Julian attributes to God the consciousness of a mother. She is, in fact, placing upon God that awareness which is characteristic of herself and her English church. "Jesus is our true Mother," she said, "and he is our Mother of mercy in taking our sensuality." This is a remarkable statement, which, while not original with Julian, has been made most evident in her writings, that Christ thinks as a woman is one way of translating what she is saying. What could she mean? God is caring, intuitive, receptive and open. As Christ was incarnate he knew what it was to live in a body, and like a pregnant woman to sense in the body the joy of new life.

Perhaps Julian could be criticized for not revealing the dark side of that motherly or feminine consciousness, which through the ages humankind has associated with death, the unpredictable and the ominous. The awareness at one and the same time of good and evil, so characteristic of a feminine mode of consciousness, is dread. Dread is a property of that sensibility of what we have already written. It is the knowledge that in nature where there is life there is death, where there is joy there is pain, and where there is knowledge there is ignorance; but ultimately, Julian tells us, there is also true hope.

Julian provides a prototype of Anglican consciousness. In order to explain how this is so I need to describe a theory — perhaps we could call it a model which challenges us to look further — of human consciousness. It is that our thinking falls into one of two patterns or modes. Traditionally these modes have been called "thinking with the right hand" and "thinking with the left hand." Right hand thinking is analytical, logical, requiring one-to-one unambiguous representations, and is characteristic of computers. Left hand thinking is intuitive, analogical, metaphorical, symbolic and characteristic of poetry, art and music. If our primary goal in thinking is to be as clear as possible with no loose ends, and the experience related to a system, we think with the right hand. This is the consciousness of science, but it only describes things as they appear to be. If our intention in thinking is to draw together as much of an experience as possible, with items unresolved and with large, nagging questions in the middle of what we have described, then we are thinking with the left hand.

Fantasy literature is an example of thinking with the left hand. The English are rather good at this kind of writing. The Inklings, a literary group that met in Oxford during World War II to criticize one another's work, produced some remarkable fantasies. They included Dorothy Sayers, who wrote mystery novels; C. S. Lewis, who wrote the Narnia chronicles and three science fiction novels; Charles Williams, who wrote novels dealing with the occult; and J. R. R. Tolkien, who is famous for the stories of the Hobbits. I would claim that there is a relationship between the gift for writing fantasy literature found among the English and that thinking with the left hand which is characteristic of Anglicanism.

We Anglicans are not given to writing great theology. There are notable exceptions, but they are difficult to remember; but when Anglicanism is at its best its liturgy, its poetry, its music and its life can create a world of wonder in which it is very easy to fall in love with God. We are much more adept at the left hand than at the right.

In this spirit the three points we made about Julian of Norwich are to be understood as characteristic of our particular way of constructing reality.

First, there is the Anglican proclivity to sensibility, the taking into account the whole of an experience — ambiguity and all. Sensibility is a difficult quality. T. S. Eliot suggested that English literature has failed to capture it since John Milton. The antidote to sensibility is common sense and if we wish to avoid living in a perpetual paradox, we insist that everything is simply a matter of common sense. Anglicanism can appear this way; but we are at our best when we acknowledge the penultimate nature of our answers to the character of God and his will for us. This modesty is often expressed as a "yes, but." "Yes, Jesus is my personal Savior, but this does not mean he is a white, upper middle class American. Yes, I believe that God has a purpose for me after death, but I am skeptical of the accounts of people who claim to have died and lived again. Yes, I believe that Christ is present in the bread and wine of the Eucharist, but this does not mean that for a particle to fall on the floor is tantamount to sacrilege."

Sensibility requires a willingness to face the darkness of chaos without romanticism. One of the reasons that Anglicanism sometimes appears merely cynical or sentimental is that we do not have the courage of our best instincts. We refuse to enter the darkness. Obscure essays from the pulpit, a fascination with the past and a fondness for empty, polite chatter are among the ways we defend ourselves from our birthright.

Sensibility is a recognition that the inexpressible nature of God can never be reduced to our categories or our simplistic notions of the divine will. This leads us to acknowledge the metaphorical nature of all religious conversion and theological discourse. For Anglicanism this recognition is coupled with the fact that God is the creator of everything that is, and that the knowledge of God requires only that we look at his handiwork. This is the second point. It is why British empiricism and its ally, American pragmatism, are very much a part of the Anglican way of thinking. For example, an Anglican approach to miracles might be that God does not run around suspending the predictable course of nature, but that there is more to God's creation than that for which our intellectual constructs can account.

Radical Protestantism and its expectation that the presence of the Holy Spirit is evident in unusual phenomena, such as speaking in tongues, finds its adherents within Anglicanism from time to time. We have no need to repudiate this. After all, Julian of Norwich, for one, exhibited some fairly unusual behavior. Our tendency is to look for a natural cause for such phenomena, not because we do not believe God speaks to us in this way, but because we believe that God makes himself known and is known in the ordinary routine of life. The Carmelite mystic, Brother Lawrence (1605-1691), who came to know God in the kitchen, is someone whom we can appreciate more than Simon Stylites (c. 340-459) sitting on a pillar for forty years.

Taken too far, of course, this fondness for the ordinary can make us very dull. Unless we enter into the world of the left hand, we will end up like a theological Scrooge (a character typical of English literature). The mystery of the ordinary will be dismissed with a "bah" and a "humbug." There is a perversity within us to carry the metaphor along, which produced in Puritan times the town crier, wandering the streets of the village on the night of December 24, calling, "No Christmas tonight." It is not that we should reduce our transcendent to the ordinary routine. It is that for the sensible consciousness the extraordinary shines through the ordinary.

Thirdly, the consciousness of Anglicanism is dominantly feminine. In medieval times England was known as the "land of Mary." The devotions that developed about the Mother of Jesus have always found a receptive home in the British Isles. This should not be too surprising in a country which counts among its greatest monarchs several queens. There is something peculiarly compatible between a feminine consciousness — be it in a man or woman — and the Anglican outlook. This is another way of speaking of the sensibility of Anglicanism, but one that will lead to some distinguishing characteristics discussed later in this book.

We often speak of Anglican "comprehensiveness." If this is a way of making relativism palatable or a means of accommodating all shades of opinion with no regard for truth, then it needs to be rejected. If by comprehensive we mean the priority of a dialectic quest over precision and immediate closure, then we are speaking of the Anglican consciousness at its best. This sense of a community of thought as opposed to a well-defined, definitive position, is what is meant by a feminine consciousness. This is why Anglicanism has never been a confessional church, as in the case of Lutheranism and Presbyterianism. It is the reason that while Puritanism, Latitudinarianism, Evangelicalism, Ultramontanism, Modernism and American Protestantism (i.e., a kind of banal "practical religion") have all been embraced by some Anglicans, none of them have been capable of comprehending the Anglican experience. They are all ultimately out of place.

A particular danger of the feminine religious consciousness is that it becomes dotty, what the dictionary defines as "amiably eccentric." In the 1980 movie "10," the role of the priest was obviously that of an Anglican. His insincere grin, his huge dog, the flatulent, ancient housekeeper, his inane conversation, the grossly lighted portrait of himself in vestments and his terrible music were all a caricature of the dotty Anglican. It is the same genre as the novels of Anthony Trollope.

Feminine consciousness possesses a darkness, as well as a light, and it is this which protects itself against amiable eccentricity. It is helpful to keep in mind that Mother of God was the person who held both the infant at Bethlehem and the crucified body of the dead Savior. The angels and demons inhabit the awareness of reality, and herein lies the ability to speak to people in the very depths of their souls. The Puritan Richard Baxter (1615-1691) reminded us that "Christ leads us through no darker rooms than he has gone before," and if we are not aware of those dark rooms we are missing the point. Julian put it this way. "For our sin is so foul and so horrible that our Lord in his courtesy will not reveal it to us except by the light of his mercy."

The form of our consciousness obviously shapes what we make of our experience. This initial chapter has far-reaching implications, therefore, for the rest of this book the reader needs to carry the awareness of this particular outlook with him or her as the exploration proceeds in the subsequent chapters. It will enable, explicitly or implicitly, much to come clear.

Chapter Two

Authority in the Church

One of the fundamental questions people ask as they seek to understand their experience is: "Is what I think it is true?" If I say that the earth revolves about the sun rather than the other way around, I can rightly be asked how I know that is true. In this case, I would appeal to scientific observation, requiring hypothesis, experimentation and proof. This would be my authority. Not everyone has the time to test every statement as to its truth, and furthermore, not every claim to truth is subject to scientific verification. There is no way that by sense observation, for example, I can prove that it is wrong to tell a lie. I have to appeal to another kind of authority.

This leads to the question of religious authority. How do I know what people say God is like is true? What is my authority? The Roman Catholic Church for most of its history has been refining the idea that when the Bishop of Rome, the Pope, speaks *ex cathedra* (literally "from his chair" or "throne") on matters of faith and morals he is infallible. This was finally defined at the First Vatican Council in 1869-1870. Classical Protestantism — i.e., Lutheranism and the Reformed tradition — has taught from the sixteenth century that the individual reading his Bible is inspired by the Holy Spirit. Radical Protestantism has relied more on the direct inspiration of the Holy Spirit. These three positions are answers to the question: What is my authority?

None of these positions represent the answer of the Anglican Communion, although all three can find representation among us.

9

For the classical Anglican point of view on authority we can turn to the enigmatic figure of Richard Hooker (1554-1600).

Hooker was reared near Exeter in England and was spotted early as a bright young man. He studied at Oxford, was ordained, and spent most of his life preaching and writing. Apparently he was not the kind of person that stood out in a crowd and he probably made a dull dinner partner. Isaac Walton even averred that his wife, Joan Churchman, was rather dowdy. Hooker himself was appointed to several livings — i.e., received the income of a parish as vicar — but never occupied them, staying rather in the London area or near Canterbury in order to serve the controversial needs of the Church of England.

No matter what his personality might have been, Hooker was the supreme apologist for the Elizabethan settlement. Briefly, the Elizabethan settlement refers to the principles by which Anglicanism was established independent of the Pope. Anglicanism does not think of itself as "founded" by Henry VIII (1491-1547) or even by Elizabeth I (1533-1603). As Hooker did, we think of the Church of England as the Catholic Church in England, separated from Roman jurisdiction when Elizabeth I became queen in 1558. Elizabeth followed her half-sister, Mary (1516-1558) who had restored the Church of England to Roman rule after their half-brother, Edward VI's death. The question that faced Richard Hooker was to state clearly what that meant for the Church in England to be separate from Rome.

Hooker answered this question in a running controversy with those persons in England committed to the Reformed tradition, of which John Calvin (1509-1564) was the progenitor. Calvin was the most astute theologian of the continental reformers. He shaped a theology and church polity which was clear and appealing to sixteenth century northern Europeans, including many Englishmen. His followers in England were known as the Puritans, the same people who settled in Massachusetts. Our problem as American Anglicans is that our culture holds the Puritans as heroes. To the Church of England they were defectors and even sometimes heretics.

This conflict in points of view is illustrated by the story a bishop of my acquaintance recounts. His son came home from school one day following the traditional Thanksgiving festival. My friend was startled to see him dressed as a Pilgrim Father. He remarked, somewhat in jest, "Why are you dressed as the enemy?" The little boy, justifiably confused having thought his father would be proud of him, burst into tears.

Hooker as well considered Puritans the opposition, if not the enemy. We cannot go into all of Hooker's thought at this point, but it is important to understand what he said about authority. The Puritans taught that the Scriptures provided a certainty that transcended all other certainty, including reason, which reason they wished to confine to "science" (i.e., all forms of human learning). They believed that the Scriptures must be read for themselves and devoid of subsequent interpretation, namely, tradition. Hooker's answer to this was that the Scriptures were read apart from reason and tradition and were subject to all kinds of private interpretations, which would of necessity be biased.

Hence, Hooker articulates for Anglicanism its answer to the question of what is our authority. Our authority is the association of Scripture, tradition and reason. Subsequent commentators have spoken of this as a "three-legged stool." If one removes a leg, any leg, the stool topples.

The threefold nature of authority — Scripture, tradition and reason — is not original with Hooker; but sixteenth century Anglicanism felt no compulsion to make claims of originality, since it conceived of itself as the continuing Catholic Church in England. This same notion of authority can be found in the teachings of Thomas Aquinas (1225-1274), a prominent theologian. It is certainly consistent with Augustine (354-430). It is, in fact, how any theologian — including those who argue against it — thinks. The theologian consults the texts, he sees what others have said, and he concludes in the light of the present understanding of reality what is the reasonable interpretation.

The balance of this chapter is a commentary on this principle of authority.

First, I wish to begin not with Scripture, but with what is most controversial, namely reason. Lest the reader concludes that the centrality of reason contradicts the point made about thinking with the left hand in the previous chapter, it needs to be understood that reason is more than that of analysis or logic. It refers to the power of the human mind to discern truth and this can be intuitive as well as rational.

Hooker believed that the cosmos was an unfolding of the mind of God in a hierarchy of orders or structures. This means that all of creation participates to a degree in the mind of God, including humanity. The reason of God reaches into the mind of humanity or is placed there like a "seed." To abide with God is for God's grace to illumine our reason until it fully participates in the divine reason. This is found in Greek philosophy, and is clearly stated for the Christian in the fourth century by Gregory of Nyssa (330-395), who says our guardian angel is a brother to our intellect. Paul apparently had this in mind when he wrote, "My knowledge now is partial; then it will be whole, like God's knowledge of me." (I Corinthians 13:12). This is all a way of saying that the created order reflects the mind of God, which is discernable to human reason.

Hooker argued this as any person of his times would beginning with the nature of God and moving then to humanity. God is a reasonable creator, he said, and therefore this is evident in what he creates. We today turn this around and say that the mind is the only way we have of transcending our own personal limitations and of making contact with God. In fact, the first thing we attribute to God is mentality. We conclude that God thinks. In this way we begin with humanity and move to God, but like Hooker we believe that by means of our reason we participate in the mind of God.

This is the basis for what is called natural theology. Natural theology holds that humankind can know God to a degree by observing nature, i.e., creation (including ourselves). It is the basis for believing that non-Christians have a certain knowledge of God. It is the reason why Anglicanism does not reject the human sciences, such as biology, geology, psychology, sociology, anthropology, as sources of the knowledge of God. The general principle is, we believe, that there is a continuity between nature and supernature. It is not to say that by the power of our reason we can come to a saving (i.e., one that makes us whole) knowledge of God. Revelation is necessary, as we shall see. Furthermore, we are brought into relationship with God by divine initiative, not by our efforts. The natural world in our thinking is not set over against the divine world. There is no radical discontinuity between God and his creation. Another way of putting this is to say that, contrary to the Reformed tradition, we emphasize the immanence of God as well as his transcendence.

This commitment to reason is perhaps most evident in our attitude toward the "free market place of ideas." Tests of orthodoxy, heresy trial, censorship of thought and such are generally alien to the Anglican ethos. Our belief is that a sincere pursuit of truth, done collaboratively, ultimately opens us to the mind of God. It is a spiritual exercise, to which God speaks for those willing to hear. For example, if I pursue rationally the study of psychology I believe that it will ultimately lead me to a deeper knowledge of God.

Secondly, in regard to the Scriptures, I will want only to speak to their authority in association with reason and tradition.

God's revelation is his self-disclosure. The best analogy of God's revelation is what occurs between two lovers. It is a personal sharing at the deepest possible level. Paul speaks of the relationship between Christ and the church as the relationship between a husband and wife (Ephesians 5:23-33). The Bible is the church's book and is the record of the personal revelation of God to humanity. The canon of Scripture — i.e., the thirty-nine books of the Old Testament, the fourteen of the Apocrypha and the twenty-seven of the New Testament — is the canon not because of any intrinsic quality of those books, but because the church says it is the canon.

The word "canon" comes from the Latin, meaning something by which you measure (e.g., a twelve-inch ruler). So the canon of Scripture is the standard, prescribed by the church, by which the belief of the church is confronted and measured. It is the normative source for understanding God's revelation. What is essential to comprehending God's ways with humanity is there. All Christian teaching and reflection begins there. This is why the Anglican Church has always taught that nothing should be taught contrary to Scripture.

To say that nothing should be taught contrary to Scripture is very different, however, from saying that only what is in Scripture shall be taught. Often Protestantism implies, if not expressly affirms, the latter. This is particularly a problem when Scripture is thought to transcend reason. People get into all kinds of binds. Some handle snakes and drink poison on the authority of the later ending of Mark's Gospel, while others will not allow the use of pipe organs in worship because the Scripture makes no mention of them. A more subtle effort is the attempt to develop a New Testament form of church government, such as Hooker's adversaries claimed to do (i.e., Presbyterianism).

Scripture for the Anglican is a fundamental source of authority for the church; but apart from reason it is dangerous. It becomes the mirror for the misdirected person to project his or her own opinions and give them the authority of God. The sin of schism is the result.

Thirdly, the Scripture must also be read in the awareness that everyone embodies his or her past and community, that is, their tradition. We cannot escape it. Hooker was skeptical of Puritan individualism, which seemed to miss this truth. The reading of Scripture is something to be done collectively in the light of the tradition. In fact, one way of thinking of the Scriptures is as normative tradition.

"To tradition" means to pass down from generation to generation within the community the church's lore, that is, her understanding of God's ways with humanity. The tradition is the product of the ongoing reflection by the church of her experience of God, and consequently it is a living, changing body of thought. It was out of this reflection that over a period of maybe three hundred years the canon of the Bible emerged, and the continuing tradition remains the context in which the Scriptures are to be interpreted.

The canon is misunderstood if it is not seen within the patterns of thought from which it came. This not only applies to what preceded the writing of the books of the Bible, but as well as to the contemporary struggle to express the community's experience and the unfolding of the implications of the canon in the centuries that followed. Hence the tradition is integral to the interpretation of Scripture.

By implication we do not believe that God's revelation of himself ends with the closing of the canon in the fourth century. The Scriptures remain normative, but God continues to reveal himself and his will in a manner that enlarges upon what is found in the Bible and in a way that is consistent with the church's understanding.

This is apparent when we think of the great dogmas of our faith. For example, there is the doctrine of the Holy Trinity. No where in the Bible does it teach that God is three persons in one nature. This understanding came several centuries later. The great Christological controversies of the fourth and fifth centuries gave birth to the doctrine that Christ is both God and man in one person or hypostasis. The meaning of the word, "hypostasis," in New Testament times was the opposite of what it meant in the fifth century, when it came to describe the person of Jesus.

In fact, it may well be that there was always a piece of the church's teaching which was carried by the tradition alongside the Scripture with no explicit mention in the text of the Bible. Here we are on more tenuous grounds; but I suspect that Christian ascetical teaching as well as the church's belief in Christ's presence in the Holy Eucharist are examples. Such areas of our belief are too much a part of the life of the church from the very beginning not to have been a part of the oral tradition all along.

There is a certain imprecision about this threefold authority which has consistently bothered students of Anglicanism. The question arises how the interaction of Scripture, tradition and reason is orchestrated to produce anything resembling an authoritative statement. The answer Anglicanism classically gives is that this is the responsibility of the church's councils. Where the church gathers to reflect on the Scriptures, in the light of the tradition, to conclude what is a reasonable position is what we mean by a council.

What constitutes a church council? There is no doubt but that we start with the four ecumenical councils of Nicea (325), Constantinople (381), Ephesus (431) and Chalcedon (451). Possibly there were two or three more. An ecumenical council is representative of the whole church. Such a council in our view has not been possible since 1054, when the church of the East finally broke with the church in the West. Since the Reformation in the sixteenth century an ecumenical council has been even more unlikely, unless like the Church of Rome one claims to be the whole church.

Yet Anglicans have continued to gather in council. The General Convention of the Episcopal Church speaks for this branch of the Anglican Communion. The Lambeth Conference, gathering every ten years and consisting now of all Anglican bishops with jurisdiction, abjures any legislative authority, but it is given authority in many ways by Anglicans throughout the world. Curiously enough, Anglican teaching in a subtle manner takes the statements of the Roman Catholic Second Vatican Council (1961-1965) as authoritative. Perhaps this is because what makes a council authoritative is the consent of the faithful to what it has declared, regardless of what that council does or does not claim for itself.

In an admittedly imprecise and sometimes clumsy manner Anglicanism sees the interaction of the threefold authority of Scripture, tradition, and reason as operating in a conciliar mode, which is ultimately a collaboration of the whole church. It is a bit like authority within the family. Somehow it rests within the parents, although not without input from the children. Not every statement made bears the same authority, and one comes to know in an intuitive way how to tell the difference. What is authoritative is what is accepted as reasonable by the whole family. One wishes for greater clarity, while knowing that such clarity would beget tyranny. Therefore, we are uncomfortably thankful for the authority as it is and accept what is vague as the price of freedom.

There is no question that this is "muddy." For example, as a member of the Executive Council of the Episcopal Church, I participated in four debates from 1977 to 1980 over whether the Episcopal Church should join the Religious Coalition for Abortion Rights. For some it appears that if one opposes joining it means they support a constitutional amendment against abortions. It happens that I am one who believes no one has the "right" to have an abortion, but I am equally against a constitutional amendment. Both the ideologues have a clear position who support the Religious Coalition on the grounds that a woman has a right to do with her body as she wishes, as do the pro-life group who argue that every abortion is murder. A more appropriate outlook, consistent with what has been said by Episcopal church councils, is that they are both wrong. The Anglican position is "muddier." No one has a right to an abortion, it says, because there is a real question about the rights of the unborn human, but there can be circumstances (e.g., rape, obvious deformity, age of mother) where an abortion is the lesser of two evils and is therefore the morally correct course to follow.

Clarity of authority should not be expected — in fact, it should be suspect — when we are attempting to make clear the infinite mind of God for the finite minds of humankind. When Anglicanism is true to its concept of authority, this apparent hesistance to say, "Thus saith the Lord!" — only to have to spend the next hundred years subtlely qualifying "what the Lord said" — is not a sign of weakness, but evidence of strength and wisdom.

Chapter Three

The Bible

Surely among the great Christians of recent times is Samuel Isaac Joseph Schereschewsky (1831-1906). He is remembered in the calendar of the 1979 *Book of Common Prayer* (October 15), but when his commemoration rolls around each year there are more jokes about the pronunciation of his name than appreciation for the incredible witness of this saint.

Born a Jew in Lithuania, from his early years he exhibited a remarkable talent for languages. While studying to become a rabbi in Germany he read the New Testament in Hebrew and came to believe that Jesus was indeed the promised Messiah. In 1854, he emigrated to the United States and began studying for the Presbyterian ministry. While in seminary, however, he concluded that Calvinistic theology and polity were not biblical and he sought to complete his studies and to be ordained in the Episcopal Church. The priest who gave him the greatest support was Theodore Lyman, then Rector of Trinity Church, Pittsburgh, and later the fourth Bishop of North Carolina. The sponsorship of Schereschewsky was probably Lyman's greatest single contribution to the church.

While at the General Convention the first Anglican Bishop of China, William J. Boone, visited the seminary and the course of Schereschewsky's life was set. Leaving in 1859 for China, his goal was to translate the Scriptures for the Chinese people. A scholar without peers, he learned Chinese while aboard ship on route to

China (it took twenty-three weeks!). From 1862 to 1875 Schereschewsky was in Peking, during which time he translated the Bible into Mandarin. He also started a translation into Mongolian, after a visit to that part of China.

In 1875 while in the United States on furlough, Schereschewsky was elected Bishop of China. He declined, principally on the grounds that he wished to finish his translation of the Mongolian Bible and do one in Easy Wenli, the classical written language of China. He was elected once again the next year, was persuaded, declined again, and repersuaded. He was ordained bishop in 1877, and served until 1883. During his episcopate he founded St. John's College in Shanghai, which later became a university and one of the great educational institutions of China. In August 1881, while living in the intense heat of Wuchang, a city to which he had come because of problems in the church, he suffered heatstroke. As a result of the very high fever he was completely paralyzed. He never fully recovered.

The remaining twenty-five years of Schereschewsky's life were spent struggling with his profound disability while translating the Scriptures into Easy Wenli and editing a reference Bible in that language. He traveled Europe and North America, seeking relief with but the one goal in mind: to complete this third translation. Often he lived in poverty. He could never sleep more than four or five hours a day. His wife, up until the last year or so nursed him through it all, while he typed out the translation with one finger. He finished his Easy Wenli translation in 1894 and then went to Japan to seek the assistance of a Chinese secretary in polishing the translation. There he lived out his final years, often in much pain, but with little complaint. His last words, most reminiscent of Dame Julian of Norwich, were, "It is well; it is very well."

Schereschewsky was not the "typical Anglican." He was neither born to it nor did he join as a result of a desire to move socially upward. He was convinced of Christianity and its Anglican expression by reading the Bible. He spent the rest of his life making the Bible available to the people of China, enduring all kinds of strange vicissitudes. This understanding and devotion to the Scriptures is in the best Anglican tradition, and Samuel Isaac Joseph Schereschewsky, a Lithuanian Jew, is the patron saint of all who in our tradition seek to live and teach the Scriptures.

I do not know what Schereschewsky's convictions were as to the nature of biblical interpretation. He was contemporary with the great Cambridge (England) triumvirate, B. F. Westcott (1828-1901), J. B. Lightfoot (1828-1889) and J. A. Hort (1828-1892), who initiated the Anglican tradition of biblical criticism. It is difficult to determine how well Schereschewsky knew their work and shared their viewpoint, although a scholar such as he must have been conversant with Westcott and Hort's Greek New Testament and the landmark commentaries of Lightfoot. Schereschewsky believed that the Bible tells a story which can be a means of God's saving grace changing the lives of those who read it. It is this understanding of the Bible that is characteristic of Anglicanism.

Our tradition understands the cultural conditioning of the books of the Bible as self-evident. Many of the books are products of an oral tradition centuries long and the result of an editorial process. Some of them are like a montage, where different versions and points of view overlay one another. Two different accounts of the same thing can appear side by side, such as the two creation stories (Genesis 1:1-2:4 and 2:5-25). Different points of view, shaped by different cultures, can be readily identified. For example, there are at least three different interpretations of the experience of Jesus in the New Testament: Palestinian Jewish, Greek Jewish and Gentile. The authors and editors of the books of the Bible were historical human beings with the normal biases we would expect.

We know there is no perfect text of the Bible and until modern times every copy of the Scriptures was done by hand. We may have fragments of manuscripts from the second century of the New Testament and whole manuscripts from the fourth (our Old Testament manuscripts are older), but no autograph copies. The fact, for example, that there was a shorter and longer ending appendixed to Mark's Gospel (Mark 16:9-20) or that the story of the woman taken in adultery was added to John's Gospel at a later date (John 7:53-8:11), for example, are questions of historical interest, but do not gainsay the authority of the Scriptures. They illustrate in a dramatic way the living form of handwritten manuscripts and the attitude of the copyists.

It is evident, as well, that the books of the Bible reflect the various literary genre of the time and that many contemporary anecdotes and aphorisms found their way into the account. For example, when Paul writes, "Bad company is the ruin of good character" (I Corinthians 15:33), he is quoting a Greek playwright, Menander (342-291 B.C.). Some of the sayings attributed to Jesus are from the common wisdom of the times. The Gospel stories of the star of the magi, the visit of the young Jesus to the Temple, and the changing of water into wine are examples of folk motifs commonly found in contemporary tales told of other heroic or divine figures. The writers had no idea that what they were doing required "all new material."

Each biblical author or editor took the material available to him and shaped it for his own purposes. In the Old Testament, Ruth and Ezra, each written about the same time, argue for different points of view as to whether or not a Jew may marry a foreigner. In the Apocrypha, II Maccabees is a more romantic version of some of the same events in I Maccabees. Matthew wrote his Gospel as the new Law, Mark constructed his account around the Messianic secret, Luke reflected on the Christ event from his philosophy of history, and John, thinking in terms of his particular Christology, used seven "signs" as a device for telling the story.

The ability to discern the way in which the Scriptures have come together to tell the story of the God who reveals himself in the history of Israel and finally in Jesus of Nazareth in no way threatens the authority of its message. It is clear indication of our understanding of the nature of biblical inspiration. We do not believe that the Bible is just like any other great literature, such as the Greek tragedies, *Beowulf,* or the plays of Shakespeare. Likewise, we do not believe that every word was dictated by God. The latter view is unreasonable. What we do believe is that within the totality of the Scriptures the story of God's love for humankind confronts us, convicts of our sin and calls us to new life. Within all the variety and human bias evident in the various passages, this story stands clear. This is what we mean by plenary inspiration as opposed to verbal inspiration.

The effect of this particular doctrine of inspiration is seen in our discomfort with the use of "proof texts," a verse or two taken out of context to "prove" a particular point. For example, Hal Lindsay, the author of *The Late Planet Earth,* claims that Revelation 17:12, which reads "The ten horns you saw are the ten kings who have yet begun to reign," is a reference to the European Common Market, and that Armageddon, the last great battle before the end of time (Revelation 16:6), is upon us. Lindsay makes no effort to take into account the stylized imagery of apocalyptic literature of that period, of which Revelation is a typical example, nor does he appreciate the historical situation in which the author finds himself in the Roman Empire. Furthermore, he seems unaware of each century's attempt to apply the number found in Revelation to themselves, with no greater or less success than he.

The Bible must be read intelligently and as whole. This is why in the Anglican Communion we do not allow ourselves to cherish our favorite book, dismissing those that do not appeal to us, and we reject efforts to pick and choose texts in our sermons that support our own interests. Instead, we read publicly during several years in the Eucharist and Daily Offices (i.e., Morning and Evening Prayer) the major percentage of the entire Bible: Old Testament, Apocrypha and New Testament. We believe that it is of the utmost importance that we hear the Bible read in course, in order that we may listen to the story in its entirety.

Our manner of listening to the Scriptures is that of an intentive intuition. We read Holy Writ with hope and the faith that as we wait upon God he will speak to us through these words. There is some technical theology in the Bible. There are specific ethical admonitions. The prevailing literary form is story and poetry, language of the left hand. It is important that this be so, since the Bible is the record of God's personal self-disclosure of himself to us. It recounts a lover's longing for the beloved; and if we are to move beyond the words to experience that love, it is the power of the story and the rhythm of the poem that will draw us there.

There is a simile in the writings of the Byzantine spiritual master, Simeon the New Theologian (949-1022) — the "old theologian" in the Byzantine church was Gregory of Nazianzus (330-390) — in which the Scriptures are likened to a "solid and well-secured chest." Simeon points out that you can carry the chest about with you constantly. You can memorize every word of the Holy Scriptures, but unless you know how to open that chest, you will never know the treasure within. It is the Holy Spirit working in the church that enables us to unlock the chest.

The Holy Spirit does not open the meaning of the Scriptures for us easily in a kind of lightening flash. He does it through years of pondering texts and thoughtfully drawing out their meaning. In order for God to speak to us through the Bible we must do some things which may seem to some very pedantic, which do not guarantee when accomplished that we will understand the Scriptures. Without attention to these steps, we can be sure we will not understand them.

First, we have to understand the words. What did the words mean when written? Revelation 17:12 is not speaking of the European

Common Market. Only a controversialist could come up with that absurd notion. It is equally foolish to think that Matthew in 16:18 had in mind the infallibility of the Pope. It is neither desirable nor possible for us to approach Holy Writ with an empty head, but we need to avoid as best we can reading into the words objects of reference which are alien to the period in which they were written. You cannot prove prohibition, for or against the ordination of women to the priesthood, or the superiority of the capitalist system from the Bible. Both are totally out of the ken of the times in which the words were written. There was no Christian ministerial priesthood, there was no capitalism in the first century and without alcohol to drink ancient folk would have died of thirst or disease.

Secondly, we have to understand the author. This comes through discerning what the author would be likely to think and do, given his culture and society. This means we have to understand how he builds his reality — his language, his symbols, his self-concept, his purpose in writing, his rules of truth, and so forth. Whoever first recounted the Virgin Birth, as it now appears in Matthew and Luke had no interest in parthenogenesis; he was not privy to the mind of the Mother of Jesus; and it never occurred to him that to tell that story he had to have certain eye-witness knowledge of the sex life of Joseph. He may have been recounting a "brute fact." He was certainly using a classical folk motif to convey the unique relationship of Jesus to God, which is a pivotal theological point.

Thirdly, we have to understand ourselves. The power of the Scriptures is its ability to illumine our lives. This means that we have to be reflective about our world and secure in our own place in it. There is no value in pretending we live in the first century A.D. We have to be willing to let the text call us and our pet theories into question. For example, we in Anglicanism have insisted for centuries that the threefold orders of Bishops, Priests and Deacons is of dominical institution (i.e., Jesus planned it that way). We even said so in the preface to the ordinal in the 1928 *Book of Common Prayer.* Anyone reading the Scriptures with an open mind knows this is not true — which is not to say that we want to do away with the three orders. They evolved early in the tradition and this is their authority.

Fourthly, we have to risk our interpretation within the larger dialogue. The Scriptures are not in our view a matter for private interpretation. When this is the case we are too ready to settle for half-baked answers. The exploration of the Bible should evoke questions whose answers evoke even more questions. This happens as we share our insights into Holy Writ and allow our interpretation to be challenged by others. The process is one that calls us into new understandings and never lets us think that we have exhausted the meaning of the Scriptures for our times.

It is clear that in the Anglican tradition that the authority of the Bible is without question, but that hearing what the Bible says is not a simple matter. Its message is one that is fresh and telling today as it was two thousand years ago. Yet it is so difficult for us to hear that message, and it is only when we probe its mysteries and let ourselves be touched by it that the Word is heard. This is why the Bible is the church's book and the task of the church is to enable the Scriptures to be heard as good news, calling us to see the world in a new way in which God is present bringing us to wholeness.

When I was a very new priest I served a small congregation of humble, sincere folk. They had inherited a tradition where the Bible was bad news. On one occasion I called on a man who was out of work. As I came into the living room he looked up at me with shame written all over his face. "Preacher," he said, "you've caught me in a great sin." I noticed his Bible on the table beside the sofa and a can of beer by his side on the floor. I asked what the sin might be and this poor man, not knowing whether he could feed his family or pay the rent, unburdened himself of his great sin. "I was reading the Bible, preacher, but at the same time I was drinking a beer."

How tragic it is when the Scriptures are used as a straitjacket to the human spirit. If Anglicanism is true to itself it will lift the burden of such futile guilt from people and help them see in Scripture the promise of God to an oppressed people. The majesty of the Word will dismiss the trivia of Pietism and lay before us a hope in the face of the despair that threatens to overwhelm us. Certainly this is what Samuel Schereschewsky sought to do in bringing the Scriptures to the people of China.

Schereschewsky was chained by his affliction, but his love of Scripture his spirit saved. He said of himself, "I have sat in this chair for over twenty years. It seemed very hard at first. But God knew best. He kept me for the work for which I was best fitted." Robert Cooper captures the spirit of the saint in these words.

I.

Something far greater than Jonah is there.
Russian Jew American Christian Chinaman
Yoked twenty years and more to your chair.
Who can bear to hear that this is God's plan?

II.

"Eli! Master! I heard you calling me
From the doughy loins of my warm mother."
It was the voice of God that would not let me be
When night closed and struck me like a wrathful father.

"Ishmael, I hear you still in the desert places.
I am Isaac, son of promise. Remember me now
Carpentered to this chair by your God who grimaces
In Jew-faced Jesus. (Before him gentiles will bow.)"

Joseph is my name also. I am God's cuckold.
I was unswayed by the hot wife of Potiphar
I conquered her, and all of Egypt's grain rolled
Forth to become God's hard loaves on earth's altar.

I am your wheat, O my God in heaven
Sown in Russia milled in the U.S.A
Baked in a world away with Chinese leaven.
Myriads will rise up from me on your great day.

I was content at last to be your lifelong joke
To offer at your table my broken old crust
To learn to be consumed in bearing your light yoke
To sit those long years in China long enough to trust

That I have seen the ways your bent things praise
How you laughed me straight through all your days.

Chapter Four

The Incarnation

Paul Tillich (1886-1965), a distinguished German—American theologian, said on several occasions that the doctrine of the Incarnation was the "Anglican heresy." Tillich was trained in the tradition of German Idealism and never really got over it. He found it very difficult to conceive of God, who is pure spirit or thought as "captured" in the physical world. For him in all his brilliance God was not to be found in the particularity of the concrete.

There are several Anglicans whose life and thought witness to the Incarnation, which is in fact a central doctrine to Anglicanism. Hugh Scott Holland (1847-1918), Charles Gore (1853-1932) and William Temple (1881-1944) leap to mind. I prefer to reflect on the figure of William Porcher DuBose (1836-1918) for one reason, if for none other. He has a fascination for me as my distant predecessor as Dean of the School of Theology of the University of the South in Sewanee, Tennessee. This in itself is sufficient cause for me to choose him, but there are other reasons. Among them is the fact that he is probably the most original theologian the Episcopal church has produced. I also find him something of a fascinating enigma.

Dubose was the son of an old, wealthy and aristocratic South Carolina family. His heritage was French Huguenot, but his ancestors had long since become Anglican. There is no evidence that his family or he held anything but the prevailing socio-political viewpoint of their class in South Carolina at the time of the Civil

War. DuBose served as a line officer during the first couple of years of that war and was wounded on several occasions. Many of his family and friends were killed, as would be expected among an aristocratic people bound by duty.

Yet DuBose had long felt a call to the priesthood, which he answered in the midst of the war. He had been previously educated at the Citadel — a military education was considered highly desirable for the Southern gentleman — and the University of Virginia. He had done one and one-half years at a diocesan school prior to 1861 and the firing on Fort Sumter. This was his formal education. Yet after a few years in the parish ministry he was invited in 1871 to Sewanee, Tennessee, to become Professor of Moral Philosophy at the struggling University of the South and he never left. He was the founder and second dean of the School of Theology, but more importantly, wrote seven books and numerous articles which reveal a profound theological mind. He is appreciated more in England than by his fellow Americans, perhaps because of the prejudice which still lingers in this country against Southern scholarship.

The fascinating thing about DuBose is that an account of his life, *An Apostle of Reality,* written by his nephew, Theodore DuBose Bratton, evokes the images of a culture that is oppressive and narrow. DuBose lived in a world clinging to the cultural ideals of a South, whose values seemed to be a combination of the novels of Sir Walter Scott and a plantation economy. For example, the long break at the University of the South took place in the winter, not the summer, probably because the winters are thoroughly unpleasant on the Cumberland Plateau. One reason given in Sewanee rhetoric for this was that every Southern gentleman had to have the occasion to hunt. The world of DuBose was racist and sexist. Blacks were not allowed at the University and were considered to be servants chosen by divine providence. DuBose himself was tended until his death by his two maiden daughters and everyone seemed to think this was an appropriate sacrifice on their part.

DuBose was a curious, creative exemplar of this culture. The Incarnation was central for him. In words very like those of Irenaeus (130-200), he wrote, "I see in Jesus not only the supreme act of humility in God, but the supreme act of humanity in God." He saw in our Lord a human nature more human than our own. He spoke of this in terms of breadth and depth. He was anything but narrow. Life was for DuBose most precious. Everything we do, he says, is for life — not the other way around — and life is most manifest in Christ.

With this in mind, I recall an anecdote told about DuBose. In America at this time there was much talk concerning Satan and the evils of sin. Someone commented to DuBose that in *The Soteriology of the New Testament,* perhaps his best known work, he mentioned Satan only once. This in itself certainly set him apart from the average preacher of his day. DuBose laughed at this comment and added, "I hope I spoke of him kindly." As a matter of fact, he did. The Southern mind, when it cuts through all the romanticism, knows that the angels and demons live in close proximity to one another.

The understanding of the play of light and darkness within creation and God himself is important if we are to embrace the Incarnation for what it can mean. DuBose was one who had seen the horror of war, he had experienced the death of many whom he loved, and he lived in relative poverty. Yet he could affirm that God is life, this very life which sometimes appeared so evil. In fact, it seemed that in the very acknowledgement of that evil grace flowed into his mind and heart. This is a mystery, but so is the Incarnation.

We will never plumb the full meaning of God's purpose in becoming humanity, but there are implications of the Incarnation to which we need to point.

First, the Incarnation means that God created everything that is. This is the beginning point of Christian belief for the Anglican: the doctrine of creation. The Incarnation is the ultimate act of creation, and if humanity had never sinned God would have become flesh. The material world is good. As DuBose wrote, "The whole creation is one and means one thing . . . life." Christ is the word of God, God's self-expression, and he is the rational principle within all of life. To know creation is to know God for those who can look beyond the landscape to the inner reality.

There is a real risk that this contemplation of creation, which is consistent with Christianity if understood rightly, can become pantheism. Pantheism identifies God with the totality of nature. The notion that "God is in the sunset" is a variety of paganism; and, whereas we could all profit from a dash of paganism every now and then, it can easily become excessive. Panentheism, the belief that all creation is in God but God is infinitely one, is a more classically Christian belief.

The protection against pantheism lies in the ability to see the purpose of God working in and through creation, and yet incomplete in and not infrequently thwarted by nature. Alfred North Whitehead (1861-1947), approximately the age of DuBose's son, was an English philosopher who developed the notion of panentheism. Whitehead taught that God both has an absolute vision for his creation and is in some ways becoming in his creation. This is called process theology. DuBose anticipated him and other notables in process thought, such as Teilhard de Chardin (1881-1955), the remarkable Jesuit theologian, by a generation. He writes:

> The law of all life, from the lowest up, is that nothing is made out of hand, but that everything in a sense makes itself by its own reactions upon other things. So life through perpetual strife with environment makes itself and rises in the scale of being only through its own victories over environment. There is no reason in itself why this should be so in the lower stages of evolution. The reason emerges and becomes apparent only in the final stage, in the production of that spiritual activity which *must* be self-activity in order to be itself.

The majesty of this statement is striking. It renders insignificant those who struggle against the great discoveries of science and affirms that in the very brokenness of creation we see the manifest presence of God. The principle of reason (the Greek is logos) is, of course, the Christ, as he is identified in the opening of the Fourth Gospel.

The "final stage" of which DuBose speaks is, of course, the birth of humanity. The image of God in humankind is the presence there of the logos of God, the ability to act in a self-conscious or reflective way, drawing on the past and anticipating the future. We do not believe that this is ever totally destroyed in us. How can we know when we are "irrational" if we do not contrast with what we know is "rational?"

Secondly, the Incarnation means that sin cannot be explained by identifying it with matter or the physical world. Anglicans have suffered much silly abuse to the effect that we are "weak on sin" because we like to dance, play cards, drink alcoholic beverages and admire the human body. Of course, this is nonsense and it does not deserve serious reply, if it were not indicative of the Manicheanism that always "lurks at the door of Christianity." Manicheanism is a religion which explained evil by dividing the world into spirit and matter. Spirit is good, it said, and matter is evil; so we avoid matter. The trap is easy to fall into. No less a theologian like Augustine of Hippo (354-430) confessed that he would have ascended to God but that he was weighed down by his body. This was no mere picture of speech for him and he could argue for it from Paul, the Apostle. The Manichean explanation of evil fails to take into account that everything is in God, and if we defend ourselves from everything we shut out God.

Anglicanism believes that sin is in the person or the community. With the ability to reason comes the ability to sin. As DuBose said, "Sin is of all things in the world a personal matter. It is the thing in the world the most independent of God Himself, and is independent of him to the point of contradiction." Because of this sin is a far more complex issue than many people realize. For example, the sin in the disease of alcoholism is often found in the people who conspire to protect the alcoholic from facing his illness rather than in the alcoholic himself.

Sin is rebellion against God. It is our refusal to serve with God as co-creators, partners in bringing to fulfillment his vision for creation. When we impose upon each other and the world in general our personal purposes, with no concern for God, then we sin. Often catechetical instruction will raise the question of the "root sin." I was brought up, to think it is pride, putting myself in place of God. I have heard it is selfishness, thinking of myself first. It could just as well be exploitation, the use of other people and the world's resources for my own ends. Pride, selfishness and exploitation are all sins against that partnership for which God created us and which he announced in his Incarnation.

Sin as Paul points out is the violation of the law. The law is God's revealed purpose for creation. It is inevitable that people will violate that purpose. We all sin. The issue lies in our continued, intentional action contrary to God's law. Currently moral theologians distinguish between these two understandings of sin by calling the former objective sin and the latter subjective sin. Subjective sin, which is a consistent working against the divine will, is what concerns us. It is much easier to count objective sins — particularly if they are among the "warm sins" of sex, anger and theft — but it is subjective sin that frustrates God's vision for creation and violates his Incarnation.

Thirdly, the Incarnation embraces the totality of life. It is the doctrine which undergirds the Anglican commitment to sensibility, the openness to the entire experience with all its conflict and ambiguity. It is well for us to bear in mind that another name for Satan is Lucifer, meaning the "one who brings light." The very personification of evil, our sin, can be a source of understanding ourselves before God.

This is perhaps the hardest thing for us to understand, as most of us have been reared in the simple mindedness of Pietism, but we need to try. A friend of mine was reported to me to have begun an address at a prominent seminary on his personal spiritual pilgrimage with these words: "Life is like walking at night barefoot through a barnyard of chicken shit." I gather from what was told me this was the most memorable moment of his week with these folks. It cut through so much of the posturing of which we Christians are capable. It pointed to the Gospel, because if anyone did just this — walk at night barefoot through a barnyard of chicken shit — it was Jesus. If we do not understand then we do not understand the Incarnation, much less its culminating moment in the Passion. If we shrink from those words, can we accept the wholeness offered in the Cross?

This is what the Cross is all about: Christ's passage into the darkness we call Hell. It was not an abstraction, it was not play-acting, it was nothing except a confrontation with the terror of nothingness both within and without. If any of the so-called "seven words from the Cross" are in truth what Jesus said, the most likely was his saying, "My God, my God, why hast thou forsaken me?" (Mark 15:34) He was not merely piously reciting psalms: he was staring into the face of evil. It was an authentic cry of pain, that echoes around the world again and again, and from the supreme source of incarnation springs the hope of humankind.

We all have our favorite books to which we return again and again. One of mine is Thomas Merton's *Contemplative Prayer.* Merton was not an Anglican during most of his adult life, but I like to think he never completely lost his Anglican roots. What we are describing here as a fruit of the Incarnation he calls dread, and defines it as "this silence, this listening, this questioning, this humble and courageous exposure to what the world ignores about itself — both good and evil." The Incarnation teaches us to live into the fecundity of dread.

What we are discussing is the mystery of God's darkness. I do not mean to equate darkness with evil, although neither do I intend to exclude the possibility of a relationship. It is true that the Incarnation declares that God became entirely human and that darkness which is in us must be in God. The problem of evil is not solved by saying that the evil is the absence of good. We know better. Nor is the problem of evil solved by placing outside God a piece of what is. This becomes a dualism, which destroys the belief that God is the creator of all. So a radical incarnationalism leaves us with the ambiguity, which as all ambiguities has a power to draw us deeper into the mystery of God. The way to wholeness lies through evil, armed with the cross of Christ.

The danger in Anglicanism's emphasis upon the Incarnation is what happens when we hold to the doctrine, but sanitize its implications. God becomes, for example, a southern gentleman.

One of the more telling stories recounted to me out of the past of the University of the South was the occasion on which two members of the seminary faculty were locked in battle over the practice of auricular confession. This was when this was still a matter of heated debate in the church. Word got out that one of the two was hearing the seminarians' confessions and he received a summons to see the Vice-Chancellor of the university (the title given the president of the institution), who at that time was also a priest. The faculty member was asked if this were true — that he was hearing confessions — and when he replied that it was indeed the fact, the Vice-Chancellor could only say, "No southern gentleman would think of confessing his sins."

Whether or not this particular story is apocryphal, it is not out of character for a debased Anglicanism, which confuses cultural ideals and values with the mind of God. The doctrine of the Incarnation supports the conviction that Christ transforms culture, he is not a projection of the culture. Whenever we allow ourselves a certain smugness and complacency, when the church becomes predictable and comfortable, then we can be assured that we are falling into the illusion that God loves Anglicans more than anyone else. Our religion then becomes very mushy and we encourage clergy who are dilettantes and laity who are bigots. It is a disease which has cursed us from the beginning in England and knows every corner of the church.

If we are true to radical incarnationalism, then our religion keeps us on edge. We cannot escape the terror of the darkness within and we know that the only remedy to evil is the Cross of the Christ. The Incarnation, God's becoming a servant to be one of us, is a sacrifice, of which Christ's Passion is the moment of fulfillment. We need to remember that for us the church building is a shelter over an altar and an altar is a place of sacrifice. There we re-present Christ's sacrifice until he comes and there we sacrifice our most cherished assurances that what we bring to God somehow enhances the Godhead.

I can imagine William Porcher DuBose through all those forty-seven years he lived at Sewanee, where the old aristocracy had gone to preserve ideals of the "lost cause," pondering how one can exist in such a climate and keep his grasp on the Gospel. He was no different than the rest of us, if we are discerning enough. We all want to know God and to be counted righteous. Surely, as Abraham of old, DuBose knew as we now know that God was in that place, but so was Satan. It is this awareness which never allows us to take our rest, but calls us to rise up and seek the promise. No wonder DuBose spoke kindly of Satan.

Chapter Five

Church and Sacraments

Anglicanism, like many other outlooks, is more true to itself in what it affirms than in what it denies. Often its heroes have been obscured by the controversy that has raged around them and, to a degree, in which they have been sometimes unwittingly drawn. Such is the person of Alexander Mackonochie (1827-1887), a man probably unknown to most readers.

The Anglican understanding of church and sacraments logically follows from the Incarnation. Yet in our history we have sometimes missed this connection, perhaps because we have not understood the abiding need of humankind for the incarnate presence of God among us. It is not just enough to look back in nostalgia to the first century or conjure up warm feelings about the Savior. God continues to "in flesh" his presence among us in every age.

By the end of the first third of the nineteenth century, participation in the sacramental life of the Church of England had dropped almost to a point of nonexistence. Later in the century, Mathew Arnold (1822-1888), an English poet and critic, predicted that the Church of England would die from lethargy. The cures prescribed for the obvious ills of the church in the second third of the nineteenth century were as many and varied as the theologies of those concerned for its renewal. A significant call for a recovery of life came from a group of scholars at Oxford University, principal among whom was John Henry Newman (1801-1890), Edward B. Pusey (1800-1882), John Keble (1792-1866) and Richard Froude

(1803-1836). The movement, a summons to the Church of England to claim its heritage in the church, ministry and sacraments, is inexplicably dated from Keble's sermon on July 14, 1833, in St. Mary's Church, Oxford, entitled "National Apostacy." There followed from 1833 to 1841 a series of ninety tracts setting forth the views of this group, which gave them the name Tractarians. The movement is also called the Oxford Movement.

The Oxford Movement began the Catholic revival in Anglicanism. This revival was not one movement, but a series of interrelated, developing concerns that might be described as "several movements within a symphony." The Tractarians were a curious lot. Their doctrine of humanity was Calvinistic. They were Evangelicals, who for one reason or another — their reading in the Church Fathers, the influence of the Romantic movement and its love for things medieval, their life of prayer — were awakened to the Catholic heritage of the church, ministry and sacraments. The Tractarians were not ritualists, which characterized the second movement of the Catholic revival, and they certainly were not biblical and theological critics, which marked the third and fourth movements. The third and fourth movements may be distinguished by two selections of essays by representatives of those movements; *Lux Mundi* (1889) and *Essays Catholic and Critical* (1926), respectively.

Alexander Mackonochie was a notable leader of the second movement of the Catholic revival in Anglicanism. He was a very unlikely person to occupy the center of a ritual controversy. Mackonochie was a man of little aesthetic sense, who could scarcely carry a tune. He had no specific interest in ceremony. He was ascetic and tenacious. A devoted parish priest and spiritual guide, he believed that the church is the Body of Christ and that the sacraments are the normative means of grace for the faithful Church person. Consequently, he felt it only right that the sacraments be celebrated in a manner which befitted their centrality in the Christian life.

Mackonochie came into prominence when John G. Hubbard (1805-1889), a wealthy London merchant, offered to build a parish church in a very poor area of London, known as Holborn. Mr. Hubbard was what we would call now a "Prayer Book Catholic," with strong social concerns. The parish was established and he built his church, St. Alban's the Martyr. Mackonochie became the first vicar in 1862. He was chosen as much for his deep concern for the poor of London than anything else — an attribute which char-

acterized the second movement of the Catholic revival in Anglicanism. In fact, one mark of the Catholic revival in Anglicanism has
been a theological conservatism and a social radicalism. When the
latter is lost we can assume that the former has become precious.

Mackonochie believed that the poor were particularly responsive
to the sacramental life of the church, and from the beginning he
built his ministry on that conviction. This was his downfall. From
1862 to 1865, there was an increasing ceremonial enrichment of the
liturgy at St. Alban's (e.g., the use of colored vestments, the mixed
chalice, altar lights, incense, vested choirs, etc.), which in 1876
brought the ire of the Church Association down on Mackonochie.
The Church Association was an ecclesiastical society, founded in
1865, with the intent of protecting the Church of England from
Romanism by keeping worship as drab as possible. The Church
Association for the next fifteen years dragged Mackonochie
through the civil courts, while he sought to live the life of a priest of
the church, providing its sacramental ministrations to the people of
his parish. The Church of England being established, of course,
disobedience to laws concerning ritual was an offense against the
state. It was a sordid affair, which was not helped by the unimaginative leadership of the Archbishop of Canterbury, Archibald
Campbell Tait (1811-1882), who was at heart a Presbyterian.

Mackonochie resigned his cure in 1882. Although he continued
to exercise the priesthood first at another parish and then as a curate
at St. Alban's, his health was broken by the persecution. In his
farewell sermon to the people of St. Alban's Mackonochie said,

> You do not come to church to receive knowledge, or to have
> your ears tickled with oratory. You come to church to receive
> grace. And if God has been pleased by his Holy Spirit to shed
> upon you grace in this Church, then return him thanks for
> that grace, and show your thankfulness by still worshipping
> at its altar.

A century later I would not say the same thing in the same manner
as Mackonochie. He implies that the church is a celestial "filling
station." His understanding of the church and the sacraments is
clear and expresses the authentic commitment of Anglicanism to
the Church and its sacramental life.

In 1887, while visiting friends in the country, Mackonochie
became lost on the moors and died in a sudden snowstorm. A
cenotaph was constructed in St. Alban's. The church is in the area
which suffered the greatest damage during World War II and was

destroyed in the London blitz. In 1964, I visited that parish. The church was rebuilt and the figure of its first vicar still lies there within the nave, a martyr to a doctrinal conflict we trust long resolved in his favor.

The Catholic revival in Anglicanism has always been more helpful in what it intuits rather than what it defends. When required to give an explanation of its insights it has adopted some of the worst Roman Catholic hack theology and aped seventeenth century French piety, which has obscured the profound need for us to recover the meaning of the church and the sacraments for our lives. The hindsight of a hundred years or so enables us now to take a more irenic look at that for which Mackonochie was a martyr.

The church is the primordial sacrament of Christ. No sane sacramental theology claims that God is captured within the sacraments. Christ is present throughout the world; but he is present in a particularly available and operative form in the church. It is the vocation of the church, all persons baptized into Christ, to make our Lord known to all people. It fulfills this mission not just by what it does, but more basically by what it is: the Body of Christ. When one looks into the eyes of the church, he looks in the face of Christ.

God reveals himself to us in a way in which we can know him on our terms, that is, historically (in time and space). To do this he embodies himself, because humans are essentially embodied creatures. We know the spirit of another only as that spirit encounters us and makes itself known in tangible form available to the senses. There is no way that we can conceive of a religion in which spirit communicates to spirit without the medium of physicality. Language itself — sometimes used to argue for a less material notion of the Gospel's medium — is a historical reality. A flesh and blood community of persons is the fundamental material reality for any embodiment of the Spirit, including language.

The belief that the church is the primordial sacrament of Christ is different from a doctrine of the church as the gathering of the elect, which is more in the Reformed tradition. The church as primordial sacrament is an active concept, the gathered church is a passive concept. In the former the church is a means by which God calls and redeems people. Its members have not any final assurance of wholeness, but are themselves wounded healers, bringing to others the presence of God that they themselves need. We do not believe in predestination as popularly conceived — i.e., some people are foreordained to Heaven and others to Hell before all time — but know that all humankind is potentially capable of wholeness.

The church is not synonymous with the Kingdom of God either. It is obviously a human institution, rife with sin. It is strange that some people today argue against the possibility of the church as the sacrament of Christ because it is sinful. Mackonochie's attitude offers an interesting contrast. Persecuted on all sides, required to answer to an archbishop whose theology was questionable, he never flinched from his conviction that the church he served was the Body of Christ. God does not require perfection of his creation for it to be an instrument of his salvation. If he did, we would all be in desperate straits.

The danger in this doctrine of the church is that we become spiritually smug. We confuse Anglicanism, which is a historical manifestation of the church, with the people of God themselves. Whereas we are not inclined to say we are the one, true church, we sometimes are given to acting as if we believed it. There is a truth to the ancient claim that outside the church there is no salvation, but only if this refers to the message of salvation which the church is called to proclaim. In no sense is the Anglican Communion synonymous with that message. It is its servant, judged in the light of its effectiveness in making the Gospel known.

The sacraments are the living out of the sacramentality of the church. The sacraments themselves are the sure promise of God's presence to us at the deepest level of our reality. They have evolved around these fundamental symbols of birth and death, the shared meal, the touch of blessing and sexuality from which the foundation of our world is built in our memory and action. The sacraments are to life in the church as sexual intercourse is to a marriage. They do not encompass it, they guarantee nothing, but out of them springs the possibility of lives changed by an intimacy with God at the deepest level.

The *Book of Common Prayer* defines the sacraments as those "outward and visible signs of inward and spiritual grace, given by Christ as sure and certain means by which we receive that grace." What does this definition not say? First, it does not say that a sacrament to be considered a sacrament has to have explicit scriptural warrant. It is clear that the sacraments, including Baptism and the Eucharist, are given by Christ through the church. The accounts of the institution of the Eucharist in the New Testament, for example, show clearly by their style that they are reflective of what is already going on in the church.

Secondly, the definition from the Prayer Book does not say that the grace of the sacraments is ours no matter what we do. This is no more true than we conjure up God by how we feel in the sacraments. The sacraments are "windows" to the ever present God, but the appropriation of that presence into our lives is conditional upon our receptivity or faith. If we despise the gift of God's presence, then we do so to our own loss.

One of the most futile arguments that has wracked the Anglican Communion is the number of sacraments. There is no merit in counting! Knowing the number of sacraments gives us control, but blocks that thinking with the left hand which is foremost in comprehending the sacramental life. Without question, the Christian life is built upon Baptism and the Eucharist. They are as essential to our life in the church as mutual consent and ongoing sexual union are to a marriage — and more so. As the history of the church has unfolded, we have discovered as well the sacramental efficacy of Confirmation, Reconciliation, Marriage, Unction and Orders. Provision is made for all of these in our *Book of Common Prayer*.

For these seven sacraments we have developed a theology which, as the church prescribes, defines the proper minister, matter, form (i.e., words), subject or recipient and intention of each one. We have spoken of the validity and the efficacy of the sacraments. Validity stipulates the fulfillment of the objective criteria, efficacy reflects upon the fulfillment of the subjective criteria. All this is good and helpful, but it does not imprison God within a number nor does it mean that everyone of us does not come into sacramental union with the divine in other ways.

The world is sacramental. The sacraments of the church lie at one end of a continuum of varying possibility of the physical world employed symbolically as being an instrument for our coming into the presence of the God who is there in his creation all along. One of the most graceful experiences of my life was washing the feet on Maundy Thursday of a little girl whom I knew to be incurably and terminally ill. I presided at her memorial eucharist five months later. This for me was a profound sacramental moment.

At the heart of the church's sacramental theology, however, is the participation by means of these symbols — water, bread and wine — in the Passion of Christ. In this way we are confronted with the reality of Christ's Incarnation at its supreme moment of offering: his death and resurrection. This is what makes Baptism and the Eucharist so central to our life as Christians: they make present in the current moment the Passion of Christ.

Baptism lies at the root of the church's sacramental life. Principal among its several meanings is the participation in the death and resurrection of Christ. In the Thanksgiving over the water in the baptismal office we read, "In it (the baptismal water) we are buried with Christ in his death. By it we share in his resurrection." Baptism is the initiation of the Christian, by means of which we come into the family of God. From Baptism the rest of the Christian life flows. Martin Luther (1483-1546), the great German reformer, reminded himself whenever he was faced with temptation or despair, "I am baptized." No one can take that relationship with God from us. We are his sons and daughters forever.

Two things should be quickly noted. First, Baptism brings us into the ministry of the church. By virtue of our initiation we are instruments of God's creation, sent to proclaim the good news. This is why in the Anglican Communion we do not speak of the ordained clergy exclusively as "ministers." We are all ministers by virtue of our baptism.

Secondly, we baptize infants in Anglicanism because we believe that we are our community. We make commitment for one another throughout life. It is only right that this include this most important commitment and that the community of faith speak for us. Naive individualism thinks we must wait until someone "makes that decision for himself." No one makes decisions alone. Confirmation is the way to "own" our commitment, which is another matter. In Baptism we initiate it as we begin everything within our community.

The Holy Eucharist is the food of the saints. It makes present the sacrifice of Christ on behalf of all people. This sacrifice, often has secondary interpretations added; such as the belief in vicarious atonement. Anglicanism has never adopted one theory of the Passion as opposed to others. The basic meaning of Christ's sacrifice, which we do believe, is that God's offer of freedom becomes actualized in Jesus and fulfilled in his death and resurrection. We accept that gift in our participation in Christ's sacrifice. He is the cause of our freedom. The Eucharist re-presents, as Paul reminds us (I Corinthians 11:26), this sacrifice; and we, by our participation, share in the effects of Christ's sacrifice.

If there is a difference of interpretation among the traditions of classical Christianity — and it seems less and less — it would be that Anglicanism believes that in the Eucharist God makes present what was in the past, whereas others may think that in the Eucharist we look back in the present to what is still only in the past, which is nostalgia. Our teaching concerning the real presence of Christ in the Eucharist is related to our conviction. Christ is present symbolically, which is to say that he is truly here, but perceived as we think with the left hand. His presence is a mystery as is the Incarnation itself. Explanations of how Christ could be present are efforts to think with the right hand, which is alien to an Anglican approach.

The next chapter will be a continuation of this discussion, as we consider the liturgy. There must be a close relationship between the sacraments and the form in which we celebrate them together as the people of God.

Chapter Six

The Liturgy

Much of the misinformation that surrounds Anglicanism is a product of the ignorance of our own history. Anglicanism as we know it has very little to do with Henry VIII (1491-1547) and his various wives — as fascinating as that may be. What has shaped its last four hundred years or so was Elizabeth I's efforts to give meaning to a reformed Catholicism, which was neither Roman nor Protestant (in the strict sense of Reformed or Lutheran). She went about doing this by passing several acts through Parliament, which makes for much duller reading than Henry VIII's wives.

The Elizabethan Settlement has to do with uniformity of worship and authority of government. The latter, which outlined the relationship of the crown, parliament and the two convocations of Canterbury and York, was peculiar to England and, unfortunately, was not sustained in the seventeenth century, which failure has been a source of problems in the Church of England ever since. The former still prevails in one form or another and is particularly characteristic of Anglicanism. Its contemporary form is that we expect worship in the Anglican Communion to conform universally to that edition of the *Book of Common Prayer* as is authorized in a given province of our communion.

Elizabeth herself said that she was not interested in poking around in the conscience of people, but she expected outward conformity. We still live in this spirit. The Act of Uniformity of 1559 applied to clergy and laity alike, and it lives on in our expectation that every practicing Anglican will be in church on Sundays and Holy Days to worship God according to the use of the *Book of Common Prayer.* It does not take much imagination to realize that this cardinal principal has set the tone of our life together.

An important effect of Anglicanism's passion for the *Book of Common Prayer* has been that those persons whose commitment and learning have shaped the evolution of the various editions of that Prayer Book have loomed large in our history (e.g., Thomas Cranmer (1489-1556), Gilbert Sheldon (1598-1677), William White (1748-1836), Walter Frere (1863-1938), Edward Parsons (1868-1960) and Massey H. Shepherd (born 1913). If we ask the people involved in the revision of the 1979 *Book of Common Prayer* who was a seminal figure in this process, they frequently mention William Palmer Ladd (1870-1941).

Ladd was not trained in the science of liturgics. As with a number of scholars of a previous generation involved in liturgical revision, he was a church historian. This perhaps gives some credence to the charge that recent Prayer Book revision has suffered from a desire to ratify the past. Ladd in his less inspired moments did fall into this trap. He served most of his priesthood at Berkeley Divinity School in New Haven, Connecticut, first on the faculty and then for twenty-three years as dean. He was a New Englander all his life: silent, undemonstrative, clear and logical. He was a person of firm conviction, contemptuous of all intellectual hypocrisy and sham.

In reading the testimonials of Ladd shortly after his death, what strikes us is that Ladd was remembered not for his interest in liturgy, but for his social consciousness. His vita listed numerous commissions on which he served in the course of social justice. He was active in such issues as child welfare and labor. Ladd was an internationalist, who long before World War II called attention to the threat of totalitarianism. He was concerned that the United States assist the Allies early in the war.

Later in his life, Ladd was attracted by the English "Parish and People" movement, an expression of the fourth movement in the Catholic revival within Anglicanism. The "Parish and People" movement believed that a sensitive liturgy constitutes a living and active Christian community, which will witness to the world. As principal spokesman, A. G. Hebert, SSM (1886-1963) wrote on this subject, and his books were read widely in this country. Ladd brought Hebert to Berkeley to lecture, only to be disappointed to discover that Herbert's interests had gone a different direction since his books published in the mid-thirties. Ladd continued until his death, however, to reflect in their light on what constituted effective liturgy. His thoughts were shared in a column in *The Witness* and later collected in a book entitled *Prayer Book Interleaves.*

Ladd believed in the symbolic relevance of liturgy, as well as its dignity ("without that distinctive Anglican vice, stiffness") and beauty. Symbolic relevance means the ability of the liturgy to engage its participants at a level of their consciousness which awakens their sensibility. Liturgy pertains primarily to a receptive or left handed form of thought. It forms and alters the social drama which people live out, often unaware, at a fundamental level of motivation. The liturgy has the power to bring us, relatively unencumbered by social expectations, to a place where we can hear God at the depth of our being. Often people confuse good liturgy with what is sentimental, faddish or even cute. Good liturgy is more likely to be fearful and make us uncomfortable. Good feelings or a sense of security can often be the very antithesis of effective worship.

The liturgy is the church's ritual and we believe that without ritual humanity lacks a significant source of meaning in its life. Ritual is the repetitive enactment of the symbols of that event which called the community into being so that event is present now with power. As we said in the last chapter, that event for Christians is the Incarnation fulfilled in the Passion of Christ. The liturgy must be an embodiment at the heart of its form of these symbols which awaken the reality of the Passion within its participants.

Ladd was an advocate of Prayer Book revision. While he was not someone to attract friends easily, two of those most influential in the development of the 1979 *Book of Common Prayer,* Massey Shepherd and Boone Porter, drew much inspiration from him. Ladd knew that Cranmer's work as the author of the first Prayer Book in 1594 was only a beginning. Each age has to appropriate the prayer book for itself. For liturgy is an expression of the experience of God at various levels. It is like a parfait, constructed of a series of layered images. Those at the top reflect the current times, while those at the bottom contain the primordial memory of humankind. The former must change or the deep symbols will become obscured under surface anachronisms.

One example of this which Ladd never tired of recalling was the obsession in the Eucharistic rite of the 1928 *Book of Common*

Prayer with confession. In the Holy Communion, he said, it would appear that we really do not believe God can forgive us our sins. We confessed our sins, they were absolved, and we continued to declare ourselves miserable sinners. This low opinion of ourselves was a product of a sixteenth century image of humanity which no longer pertains and has been removed to a great degree in the 1979 *Book of Common Prayer.*

The Prayer Book is, of course, a living liturgy. It will always be changed to reflect the historical situation in which it is used — both time and place — but it will also frame those fundamental symbols of our faith that re-present for us the mysteries of Christ's Incarnation and Passion: the water of Baptism, the bread and wine of the Eucharist, as well as the other manifold expressions of blessing, healing, joining and forgiving.

Ladd was deeply committed to the participation of the entire congregation in the liturgy. His theory was that the reason Morning Prayer came to replace the Eucharist as the principal service of worship on Sundays was that Cranmer did a better job of making the Daily Offices participatory than he did the Eucharist. Another way of putting it, which overlaps Ladd's theory somewhat, is that the Eucharist required more effort than Morning and Evening Prayer and as theological conviction lagged and Anglicanism became lazy, the Eucharist fell into the less frequent use.

There is no question but that Anglicanism holds the Holy Eucharist to be the principal service of worship on Sunday. It is not a matter of providing "alternatives" to the Eucharist or Morning Prayer, any more than for a husband and wife reading love poetry is an "alternative" to sexual intercourse. The heart of liturgical worship for the Christian as Anglicanism sees it is the weekly remembrance of Christ's sacrifice in the Eucharist.

It is important that the Eucharist be celebrated so that it invites participation at a sensible level.

Sensibility comes through being a part of the action. It requires the inclusion of persons other than the priest in reading the lessons, offering the prayer of the faithful and in distributing the elements, but it calls for more than that. There should be times of silence to allow the people to make themselves at home in what is being said or done; and there needs to be a sense of presence on the part of the priest which does not intrude his personality and yet invites intimacy. These are ideals in Anglican worship, which should be cause for rejoicing when present rather than complaint when absent. They are difficult to achieve.

Preaching is an essential part of liturgy to Anglicans. Our intention is that the readings in the lectionary, as given to us by the church, are to be interpreted in the sermon so as to illumine the lives of their hearers. Anglican preaching has been characterized by some as boring, unenthusiastic, pedantic and uninspired. It can be all of these things, but our conception of its purpose does not require that it be any of them. It is true that we do not "preach for a decision," as is often the intention in the revivalist tradition (which includes the Methodists, Baptists, Disciples and the various Pentecostal groups). We preach for insight that requires an ability to listen and think with the left hand.

The spirit of the revivalists is not unknown among us, however. Revivalism comes from the Pietism that was brought to this land early in the eighteenth century and is associated a generation later with John Wesley (1703-1791) and George Whitefield (1714-1770). Pietism teaches the absolute authority of the Scriptures and the necessity for a personal experience of salvation. Preaching is at the center of its worship.

Where Pietism stuck in Anglicanism it is known as the Evangelical movement. It was responsible for a reawakening of Anglicanism in England at the end of the eighteenth century, which included religious education and a renewed social consciousness. Although it is difficult to generalize, it is probably fair to say that where Evangelicalism exists today in Anglicanism there is not the awareness of liturgy as the heart of our Christian life. Liturgical worship does not usually effect that dramatic, identifiable moment of knowing God's overwhelming presence, which evangelistic preaching seeks, and consequently is played down. It is also true that there are more obvious points of contact between Evangelicalism and the expectations of popular American religion, and consequently, the homogenized worship of Protestantism seeps into some Anglican parishes in this country.

Whereas Evangelicalism attempts to make the issues and answers of sixteenth and seventeenth century reformed theology normative, Ladd was very concerned that in Anglican liturgical revival we not make seventeenth century Roman Catholic practice normative. He was quick to speak out against various uncanonical or illegal liturgies that arose during the first half of this century, such as the American Missal. As he rightly pointed out, they were adaptations of the Roman Catholic Missal of Pius V (1504-1572). Those very things which Roman Catholic liturgiologists were seeking to abolish we were incorporating (e.g., the Last Gospel, noncommunicating High Mass, private devotions at the beginning of the rite).

This leads to a very important point. It is vital for us to be clear concerning the authoritative liturgy in the Anglican Communion. We cannot have "two Prayer Books," as some suggested we ought during the debate over the 1979 *Book of Common Prayer,* and we cannot have the option of choosing our own liturgy. The reason is that for us what we pray is what we believe. This is usually stated in theology in the Latin, *lex orandi lex credendi* (literally, "the law of praying is the law of believing"). Whereas some communions have their official theologians and others have their confessions, we have the *Book of Common Prayer.* Our theology arises out of our common liturgy.

The Anglican commitment to uniformity of worship is more than a matter of taste or convenience. It is a question of belief. For example, if we look at the 1979 *Book of Common Prayer* with a theological eye we will see an understanding of humanity as sinner and yet capable of longing for God. Anglicans since Pelagius, a fifth century British monk, have been given to thinking we can save ourselves; but the *Book of Common Prayer* is clear that, whereas we do not agree with Calvin that we are totally depraved — we removed from the 1928 *Book of Common Prayer* the words in the Confession "there is no health in us" — we require God's powerful presence to become whole.

Two dangers come to mind in this emphasis upon liturgy. One is that we can become precious. Ladd was not exempt from this, as I have already suggested in passing. He seemed to make overmuch of the Nonjurors, a group of church people including eight bishops who remained loyal to James II (VII) (1633-1701), when, because of his pro-Papist policies, he was forced to abdicate in the English rebellion of 1688. James II (VII) was replaced by the Calvinist William of Orange and his wife, Mary, who actually had the claim to the throne. The Nonjurors believed that to swear allegiance to William and Mary would be a violation of their previous oath to James II. They included most of the intellectual leadership of the Church of England at that time. They also held a higher doctrine of the church and the sacraments than those who took the oath to William and Mary. Because they refused to swear they were expelled from their offices in the church. Ladd apparently felt that we needed to recover their pure Anglican spirit.

This rendering of a period from the past as ideal imposes an artificial liturgy. Obviously, we draw from the past. But we must not do it in an arbitrary, uninformed or unreflective fashion. Liturgy has no purpose in itself. As is true for the Scripture, if liturgy is to live it must illumine our lives and give them meaning. Otherwise our worship becomes affected. Priests can fuss over an apparel on an amice — an oblong piece of embroidery that is attached to the soft collar of an alb — for ten minutes and then preach at the Eucharist an utterly inane sermon for five minutes. This is being precious. We have our priorities all wrong.

The other danger is that we loose confidence in the liturgy to effect the deep transformation of our peoples' symbolic world. We push for an immediate payoff, a goosy feeling they can repent as they walk out the church door. This leads to gimmickery or foolishness. I have heard it suggested that on the feast of the Ascension one might preach from a ladder leaning against the rood beam. More than one priest has ridden into his church on Palm Sunday on a donkey, which has provided much food for the local wits. There was a time in the 1960's when every church conference had to have helium-filled balloons at the closing Eucharist.

Liturgical tricks are only exceeded in bad taste by priests who confuse sloppy with sincere worship. I once knew a bishop who thought it "meaningful" to read the liturgy as if he had never seen the Prayer Book before. One priest explained to his congregation that his ill-fitting alb, his levis and muddy boots made people feel that he was "one of the people." Still another cleric justified his sanctuary manners, which left observers with the impression of a hippopotamus on locoweed, on the grounds that he was afraid of appearing effeminate.

Anglicanism takes a great risk with its insistence that liturgy is the ground of church life. This claim lays upon us the need to perform great drama, or something very close to it, every Sunday. The fact that we frequently fail is not nearly so noteworthy as the fact that so often we succeed.

Chapter Seven

The Episcopacy

The Church of England in the United States was in an unfortunate situation following the American Revolution. The first parish had been established in Jamestown in 1607 and more than 175 years later there was still no resident bishop in North America. That made life difficult for a church that required the episcopate for the ordaination of its priests. It goes without saying that no one was confirmed. There were a number of reasons why no one had been made a bishop in colonies. Prominent among them was the fear of "prelacy" and its association with the meddling of the English crown which many of the colonists had come here to escape. Another reason was the lack of imagination upon the part of the English church.

The situation after the Revolution was made difficult also by the marked tendency for Anglican priests and leading laymen in this land to have been Tory sympathizers or even collaborators. Many left after the end of the war and others were in bad odor. To a certain extent the Revolution had been the result of popular enthusiasm stirred by revivalism and the theories of intellectuals like Thomas Jefferson and George Washington, most of whom were not actually Christian in belief, much less committed Anglicans. It is misleading to suggest, as is sometimes done, that having finished writing the United States Constitution, the delegates went across the street in Philadelphia and wrote the Constitution of the Episcopal Church. Among the American

49

founding fathers, only the aristocratic Alexander Hamilton stands out as a churchman.

Anglicanism survived in the United States due to the courage and persistence of a few brave people — but just barely. The presenting problem was that someone had to think for the very first time of what it meant to be an Anglican and not a member of the Church of England outside of the United Kingdom. The clearest symptom of this was the struggle to obtain the episcopacy for the fledgling church. Samuel Seabury (1729-96), who had been a Loyalist during the Revolution, was elected Bishop of Connecticut in 1783. Because he could not now take the Oath of Allegiance to the English crown, he could not be ordained bishop by the English bishops. The problem was solved by his consecration by the bishops in Scotland — a vestige of the Nonjurors — where in part of the United Kingdom the church was not established.

William White (1748-1836) and Samuel Provoost (1742-1815), bishops of Pennsylvania and New York, respectively, were consecrated in 1787 by the English bishops, an act finally having passed Parliament which permitted this. Once that happened, there were three bishops in the United States; this number is regularly necessary for a consecration of another bishop. The Episcopal Church in the United States was not yet set on a steady course. William White had been a supporter of the Revolution and gave the Episcopal Church credence both by his person and his leadership, but Provoost was not a strong leader. He did not have much hope for the survival of the Episcopal Church. He resigned in 1801 to his farm and was followed by the saintly, but also ineffective, Benjamin Moore (1748-1816) as Bishop of New York.

What was needed was someone who could set forward the case for the historic episcopate and all that it implied for Anglicanism and challenge the church to grow. It is interesting that the name chosen by its founders for this branch of the Anglican Communion, the Protestant Episcopal Church in the United States of America, affirmed the centrality of the episcopate. We called ourselves a church which has bishops, (i.e., Episcopal), but is not Roman Catholic (which is what Protestant meant in those days rather than referring to a distinct theological outlook). James Madison (1749-1812) had been made Bishop of Virginia in 1790, but the church there found it difficult to pull itself out of either revivalism or latitudinarianism. (Latitudinarianism is an outlook, dating from the Cambridge (England) Platonists (1633-88), which outlook is indifferent to matters of doctrine, order and worship. The Cambridge Platonists held a mystical view of reason as a source of revelation.) The first bishop of North Carolina, John "Mad Jack" Ravenscroft (1772-1830), described Madison's successor, Richard Moore (1762-1841), as "no better than a Baptist," which was a fairly accurate assessment of the state of the episcopate in the South at his time (except, of course, for the eccentric Ravenscroft).

The leadership the Episcopal Church needed was provided by a contemporary of Ravenscroft, John Henry Hobart (1775-1830). Hobart was born and reared an Anglican in Christ Church, Philadelphia, where William White was rector. He studied at the University of Pennsylvania and Princeton and was ordained Deacon in 1798. He served three parishes briefly and came to Trinity Church, New York, as an assistant in 1800. He never entirely left Trinity. Nearsighted and suffering from chronic indigestion, Hobart still managed to be an eloquent preacher, a pastor, scholar and author as a priest at Trinity. In 1811, Bishop Moore suffered a stroke and Hobart was elected his assistant bishop although he was in charge in almost every way but in name, since Moore was partially paralyzed. As was the custom then, he also continued at Trinity Church.

Hobart faced a time not unlike that when James I (VI) (1566-1625), previously King of just Scotland, came to London in 1603 to become also King of England. The Puritans assumed that since James came from Presbyterian Scotland, he would now abolish the episcopacy in England. In fact, James, who believed in the divine right of kings, quickly concluded, "No bishop, no king." Now once again in the early nineteenth century there were not a few persons who wondered why the Episcopal church bothered with bishops, particularly since presbyterian polity seemed better suited to a republic. Hobart could hardly argue "no bishop, no king;" in fact, this would have confirmed the suspicions of many concerning the sympathies of the Episcopal Church. Historically, if he had looked back to the seventeenth century Caroline divines, Hobart would not have found unqualified support for insisting that bishops were essential to the church in America. There was a real question in the seventeenth century as to whether bishops were universally essential or just necessary to the Church of England. The decisions of the young Episcopal Church had much to do with resolving that uncertainty.

Hobart set about to affirm the gifts of Anglicanism by grounding his vision for the future mission of the church in a strong episcopate and an educated and devout priesthood. He argued for this in his writing, preaching and living. The first two years he was bishop the clergy of his own diocese, correctly seeing themselves under some judgement, were a vexation to him. Hobart, not only persisted, he risked his frail health by traveling extensively over his vast diocese to spread the Gospel as Anglicanism had received it. In fact, he died while visiting St. Peter's Church, Auburn, now in the Diocese of Central New York. One indication of Hobart's success was that when he became bishop there were twenty-six priests in the Diocese of New York; nineteen years later there were 133.

In 1816, Moore died and Hobart became the head of the diocese in name as well as in function. In 1817, he founded the General Theological Seminary, the first Episcopal institution for the education of priests. It is interesting that the property for this school was given at Hobart's request by Clement Moore, the son of Bishop Moore, who donated his apple orchard, fronting on the Hudson River. That same piece of property now lies between Ninth and Tenth Avenues and is bounded by Twenty-first and Twentieth Streets. The Hudson River is a block or so away. Times change, but Clement Moore will always be remembered, but not for his apple orchard. He was the author of "The Night Before Christmas."

Despite his openness to Christians of other persuasion, there is no doubt that Hobart believed that episcopacy was ordained by Christ. His advocacy of a strong episcopate extended, however, beyond simple biblical proof. This is important for us to realize, that we now know the office of bishop, as we now conceive it, evolved over several generations after Christ.

Certainly, the argument for the episcopate is not that it makes for a more efficient form of church government. Whether or not it could be more efficient, the constitution of the Episcopal Church as a result of the inordinate fear of prelacy so limited the bishops as we know them that they have relatively little real power. This is unfortunate in that we indeed do hold our bishops accountable for what they have no ability to alter. The episcopate as constituted is not, therefore, very efficient at all. Methodist bishops, who are not held nearly as accountable, have a great deal more real power, and the Methodist Church has a more efficient system.

It was after Hobart that the argument developed that bishops guarantee our participation in the true church. The Tractarians made much of Apostolic succession, by which they meant that Anglican bishops could trace by fact of ordination — the actual, physical laying on of hands, called tactual succession — their ordination back to the very Apostles. The tactual passage of the authority of the Apostles implied a "pipeline theory" of power. In other words, grace was thought to have been poured like a liquid into a pipe by our Lord and each ordination of a bishop, according to this theory, added another section of pipe to the line. This very mechanic notion of grace gave birth to the "three branch theory" of the Catholic Church; namely, that the true church has three parts: Roman, Eastern and Anglican. Obviously, the Protestants were unchurched.

Hobart argued from neither tactual succession or the three-branch theory, nor do I. The importance of the bishop to Anglican thinking cannot be understood apart from a left handed consciousness: an awareness of the profound symbolic power of the bishop. The bishop for us is the embodiment, the real symbol, of the universality of the church. We believe that as the primordial sacrament of Christ, the church must transcend the immediate time and the particular place. The church is a historical incarnation of the eternal Lord in all times and places. This truth is symbolized in the office of the bishop. The church is in and yet above cultural expressions, it stands apart from purely national interests. When one is present with the bishop, he or she is not only aware of this, he or she participates in this transhistorical reality.

What follows from this is the teaching office of the Episcopate. Historically, the bishop is the one called to preach. He speaks out of the universal experience of the church. It is the bishop who should be able to transcend the immediate situation to give us a catholic vision. The catechism in the *Book of Common Prayer* says the bishop is the one called "to guard the faith." This is an unfortunate choice of words. I assume by "faith" the Prayer Book means what is believed — faith is better thought of as the attitude or expectation, not the articles of belief — and what is believed is more dynamic than something to be guarded like lifeless gold in a bankvault. Be that as it may, from this teaching office is derived the responsibility also for the discipline of the church, the framing of her life in accordance with the principles of belief.

The symbolic function of the bishop is rightly set forth in his liturgical function. Whenever present, the bishop of the diocese is the chief liturgical officer. At Christian initiation he presides and at the Eucharist he is the chief celebrant and preaches. Yet occasionally, the congregationalism of Episcopalians creeps into even our liturgy. I have heard the diocesan bishop welcomed to a parish as "our guest." This completely misses what the liturgy proclaims; namely, that every parish church in his diocese is his parish. The rector or vicar serves there as the bishop's representative.

The importance of the bishop, to which Hobart witnessed, has been clarified in the subsequent history of Anglicanism. In the latter part of the nineteenth century, the issue of church union arose. At the General Convention of the Episcopal Church in Chicago in 1886 and two years later at the Lambeth Conference (the gathering every ten years in England under the chairmanship of the Archbishop of Canterbury of all the bishops in the Anglican Communion), four basic principles, called the Chicago-Lambeth Quadrilateral, were stated on which the Anglican Communion would approach the matter of union with another communion. Those principles are: 1) the authority of the Old and New Testaments, 2) the rule of faith found in the Apostles and Nicene Creeds, 3) the two sacraments of Baptism and the Eucharist, and 4) the historic episcopate. The seventeenth century ambiguity was now officially resolved.

This does not mean, however, that episcopacy ceased being a matter of debate in Anglicanism. The argument centers in the question of whether the episcopacy is of the *esse,* the *bene esse* or the *plene esse*; that is, does it exist for the being, the well being, or the full being of the church. If we adopt the position that it is necessary for the being of the church, we "unchurch" all those without bishops in apostolic succession. As one wag has put it, it is obviously not for the well being of the church. The position I hold is that it is for the full being of the church. This is consistent with its symbolic function.

The doctrine of the episcopacy has so preoccupied Anglicanism that we have only recently reflected on the meaning of the priesthood, yet the nature of the episcopacy raises questions concerning this second order, as well as the diaconate. The English word priest comes from the Latin and Greek for presbyter or elder. It has almost no etymological connotation for theology, but it does have a historical association with the Latin *sacerdos,* "one who offers sacrifice." During the Reformation when the sacrificial nature of the Eucharist was debated, the word priest was controversial. Yet, unlike the Reformed and Lutheran traditions we retained the notion of the ministerial priesthood awaiting a clarification that came centuries later. Now, as Anglicanism holds that the Eucharist is a re-presentation of the sacrifice of Christ, we understand the priest to be one who offers sacrifice in the sense that he or she recalls the one sufficient sacrifice of Christ until he comes again.

In the last generation, the doctrine of the ministerial priesthood has been more in question, because of the issue of the ordination of women to the priesthood. Fundamentally, the priest is one who proclaims the Word. "Word" is to be understood in a broad sense. The Word is God revealed in Christ. Proclamation involves the being and action of the priest, who is both a symbol and the bearer of the symbols. It focuses on him or her as liturgist and preacher, but includes the priest as teacher, pastor, scholar and administrator. To bless and to absolve sins are acts in which the priest proclaims the Word. An extended discussion of this doctrine of priesthood can be found in my book, *The Priest in Community* (Seabury, 1978).

The diaconate is the third order in the Anglican Communion. Like the Roman Catholics, we have remained confused about deacons for almost a thousand years. For five hundred years before that the diaconate was the order of the professionals — the teachers, the lawyers, the administrators — but about the year 1000 it began to fade in importance. There are those in the Anglican Communion today who make an eloquent plea for the revival of the diaconate, but so far their vision has not caught the imagination of the church. The diaconate remains in the minds of the majority of people a way station on route to the priesthood.

The word deacon or diaconate comes from the Greek, meaning "to serve." The diaconate is, at the very least, a symbol that at the heart of ministry lies service. All of us are called to be servants to one another, even the bishop or, one might say, most especially the bishop.

Both the priesthood and the diaconate are derivative of the episcopacy. Priests and deacons cannot reproduce their own kind. Their ministry is an extension of the bishop's. It is also true that the ministry of all three orders is an extension and focus on the ministry of the whole church. The *Book of Common Prayer* speaks of four orders, adding the laity, and notes that each represents the church to God. It is true that even the bishops do this, but this is only a half truth. The bishops and those whose orders are derived from the bishops also represent God in Christ to the church. From the Anglican viewpoint those in Holy Orders — bishops, priest and deacons — do not merely perform functions of the church. They are the embodiment of a transcendent Word. The authority flows both from the church and from God and is rendered incarnate in the life and ministry of the bishop. In this sense we agree with Ignatius (35-107), who said, "Where the bishop is, there is the church." I would only qualify his words to add "in its fullness."

The risk in this high doctrine of the episcopacy is that we use it to excuse our laziness. Because we possess the episcopate does not guarantee that we are doing the Lord's work. We in Anglicanism have for so long sustained our commitment against all kinds of attack upon the episcopate that it just may be that we have an unreasonable expectation of what bishops accomplish. There is more to being a church person than deferring to a kindly, old gentleman, whom we hold in affection so long as he does not threaten us.

There is a tendency in the American system of electing bishops — that they must obtain a majority of the votes of both the priests and the lay delegates in the diocesan convention — to look for someone who will please. The result can be mediocrity, even though the Holy Spirit has been known to surprise us and use persons elevated to the episcopate who seem to have very little talent to confront and call us to action. Too often we expect our bishops, rather than calling us into a new awareness of what it means to be the people of God, to assure us that we are all good people. There is no question of the importance of the episcopate to us. The issue is whether or not we have the courage of our convictions to elect the best to office, even when they appear to be persons who will challenge us.

One would hope that what was said of John Henry Hobart at his death might be said of every bishop. The following from his obituary in a New York newspaper rings a note that carries a sense of effective presence.

> He was, at the very heart, a Protestant Episcopalian. He approached the altar with a firm step . . . so zealous, so laborious, so undeviating was his devotion to the distinguishing principle of episcopacy, that in the American Church he became, at last, the very chief of the apostles.

Chapter Eight

Pastoral Care

Anglicans are fond of saying that we are a "pastoral church." I am not sure we really know what that means. It can be used as an excuse for not saying the hard words and risking martyrdom, or it can be a testimony to self-effacing love. This chapter is a call to live up to our self image.

A couple of illustrations of our misuse of the pastoral role come to my mind. A priest explained to several of us in the late 1950's that he only told Bible stories from the pulpit. He did not think it "pastoral" to speak to the issues of the day about which his people probably knew more than he. His parish was in rural Louisiana. A parish priest commented to me in the late 1960's, when the "new morality" was all the rage that he knew absolutely nothing about sex and would not venture to talk to his parishioners on the subject. He was more interested as he put it, in being a good pastor. He was married; I wonder how his wife felt about his ignorance of sex. A returning alumnus to our seminary suggested to some of our students that parish visitation was a waste of time. If people wanted a pastor, he explained, they knew where to find him. My experience telephoning parish priests across the land is that they are often very difficult to find.

The pastoral commitment of the Anglican tradition needs to be examined, not because the tradition is inappropriate but because we often use the label to avoid really being pastoral. I recall a young priest who had recently joined our local gathering of clergy.

We were in the habit of telling one another at these meetings how busy we had been administering the parish. There was the inevitable recounting of the telephone calls, the committee meetings, the Every Member Canvas, the bulletin publications, the building plans, and on and on *ad nauseam.* "My God," he exclaimed, "are we called to do all this? It's crap!" There was a dead silence as his elders looked at him; and then someone moved that we study what he had to say at the next meeting a month from then. His moment of prophetic utterance was lost forever in the busy-ness of a study group.

The Anglican "patron saint" of pastors is George Herbert (1593-1633), a young English aristocrat, who composed magnificent poetry as well as a book in pastoral theology and served a small country parish. He wrote about sin and death, as well as the cross and love. There is a gentleness and light to what he says; and yet in his pastoral theology he calls the priest to be faithful to his people, to visit them as one who bears in himself the wounds of Christ. The pastor, according to Herbert, is one who carries a cross so that others might bear their own cross with hope.

Herbert is the pastoral ideal whether or not his people thought of him in this manner. My illustration of pastoring is someone else, less well known and no poet of which I am aware. For personal reasons — my wife was born and reared near where she ministered — I have been fascinated by Deaconess Margaret Dudley Binns (1884-1968), who for fifty years served the church in an isolated village in the Appalachian Mountains of southwestern Virgina. She was a native of Brooklyn, New York, and a graduate of Vassar College. Young Margaret Binns married a priest, Hugh Binns, who while they were traveling to his first cure, died. Instead of going back home, she carried on his work. In 1915, having graduated from the deaconess school in New York, she followed the new railroad into Nora, Virginia, back in the remote mountains. She found there a store, an unused church belonging to the coal company and a few families. She rented a house and received permission to use the church building.

Deaconess Binns lived and died with these people. When the lumber company came in 1917, she opened a school in which she, and one other teacher hired by her, taught for sixteen years. In a number of places in the surrounding communities, including one with the wonderful name of Dismal Mountain, she established Sunday schools. She got to them by riding horseback. She was the local "doctor," teaching health care and ministering to physical needs of the people as best she could, very much in the spirit of George Herbert. When the lumbering played out the coal companies came in, and Nora was on the route of the never ending coal trains. Anyone who has visited the coal towns of the southern Appalachians knows the bleak, hopeless climate of those little isolated communities, dependent upon the coal company and its bosses. In this situation, Deaconess Binns labored until after she was eighty years old.

St. Stephen's in Nora, where Deaconess Binns worked for all those years, no longer exists. The church decided that such little congregations were no longer "viable." Of course, the church was right, if our norm of viability is the suburban parish. The school in Nora was named for her and so Deaconess Binns is still remembered in Nora and other adjoining communities in which she cared for those humble folk. More importantly, she lives in the memory of the four children she adopted. The orphans she personally raised, the people she taught to read and write, the lives she saved, and most especially in the Gospel of freedom and hope that she lived and preached.

To be truly pastoral — that is, to be a shepherd like the Great Shepherd — we need to know not only what we are doing but why we are doing it. This is the first principle of the Anglican pastoral outreach. Deaconess Binns believed in a Gospel of the incarnate Lord, who gave hope to people who had every reason to feel hopeless. They were tied to a creek bank, where they grubbed out an existence at the whim of nature and the free enterprise system. They were not even educated enough to know that this was not how it had to be. The church's mission to the Appalachians preceded Paulo Friere in Brazil and the "consciousnization" of the poor by a generation or so. Deaconess Binns knew that if the Gospel was to free them grace had to come in the form of knowledge, health and love. Jesus Christ is the Lord of all and his Lordship can only be known as life has hope in all its aspects — not just in preaching on Sunday.

The pastoral instincts of Anglicanism need to be formed as an intentional statement grounded in our theology. Our Lord came preaching "repent for the Kingdom of Heaven is at hand." This is an intentional statement revealing Jesus' theology. The theology is that God has a purpose for creation and he is active in history, bringing that purpose to pass. The intentional statement has a goal:

the Kingdom of God. What does the Kingdom look like? Perhaps, the Beatitudes describe it (Matthew 5:1-12) or it may be like the peaceable kingdom recounted in Isaiah (10:33-11:9), or some other image. The intentional statement has the objective, the means by which one arrives at the goal and it is repentance. Repentance is not just feeling sorry for our sins, but seeing the world in a new way. Jesus came to subvert our old outlook and give us new vision.

What is the goal of the Anglican pastoral intention? Is it to die and go to heaven? Perhaps, although something about that notion is profoundly unsatisfactory. The biblical imagery of a life together, the Kingdom of God, where our participation in one another and in all of nature is not thwarted by sin and the imperfection of creation, enabling our own personal wholeness, is more satisfying. The meaninglessness of suffering is subverted by the meaning of the Passion. It is a metaphor, because we do not know how to picture the end, but it has power. The goal is something we can only intuit with our left hand. Yet it is there and we believe it because we have a glimpse of the promise in Christ.

What are the strategies of the Anglican pastoral intention? It is to share an authentic love. Love is what draws humanity and God together — love as it wells up in us and as it is given to us from above. To love is to will the will of God for ourselves and the other. Such love is not primarily a feeling, much less a mere sentiment. It is a power, which when grace-full, challenges, admonishes and confronts, as well as supports, praises and comforts. Violence may not always be unloving, and anger is certainly not the opposite of love. Fear is the opposite of love and love drives our fear. If we would be pastoral, we must also be prophetic.

Anglicans do not divide the world into the sacred and the profane. We believe that love must be known and shared in every aspect of life. So politics, economics, industry, business, recreation, as well as our private lives are the arena for the pastoral concerns of the church. The Christian practices medicine, manages his business, runs the government, sells shoes, works on the assembly line, plows corn and plays baseball under the same fundamental pastoral intention as the priest functions: to awaken people to see the Kingdom of God through love that provokes repentance, a new way of awareness.

One clear implication this has for us is that the church is not isolated from the rest of life. The priest is not a professional, who does only certain procedures and pleads ignorance of everything else.

Herbert in his pastoral theology described the priest as an ambassador of Christ and then suggested some good manuals in law and medicine that the priest needed to read. It is not appropriate for most pastors today to practice medicine and law, but medicine and law or what have you are never outside the overall pastoral mission of the church.

A second principle of Anglican pastoral care is that it is sacramental. Here, I refer initially to a theological premise. It is this. Christian conversion, a turning to Christ, is the result of a marinade rather than a glaze. We are transformed by being soaked in the Gospel, rather than having it brushed on at the last minute. The sacraments are focal points of a life lived in relationship to all that conveys the humanizing grace of God in Christ. When we let them, the sacraments reach deep within the self to touch and shape those primordial images by which we live life at the deepest. The Passion of Christ becomes, in this process, the prevailing icon of all life for each of us.

The role of the sacraments has often been obscured in the church, not just the Anglican, but even the Roman Catholic, over the last four centuries. We became overly concerned about the abuses of the late Middle Ages from our analytical viewpoint and adopted an outlook which made it difficult to perceive how the sacramental life functions. This can only be resolved as we compliment the modern obsession with right hand thinking — e.g., how does it work? How is Christ present? How can an infant have faith? — with a healthy left-handed trust in the power of the symbols.

The fundamental pastoral sacraments are Reconciliation and Unction (or Healing). They have to be seen, of course, in the wider sacramental perspective of Baptism and the Eucharist.

There are two forms in the 1979 *Book of Common Prayer* for the Sacrament of Reconciliation (sometimes known as Penance or Confession). This is a sacrament of God's love. It engages our real guilt at the concrete level — "I have been selfish with my children by hanging on to them," "I have been unfaithful to my wife with a certain person," "I have cheated in my business by stealing from a given account" — so that God's forgiveness can be specific and his love can be bound to sins in a tangible, incarnate manner. This pastoral care is at the level of sensibility.

The well known Anglican saying concerning Reconciliation is that "all may confess, no one has to, and some should." My problem is that I have never met anyone who should not participate in the Sacrament of Reconciliation. John F. Fletcher (born 1905), a distinguished ethicist, once said in my hearing that in a parish where people regularly make their confession a new priest can be as effective in six months as a priest can be in six years in a parish where it is not the practice.

The Sacrament of Unction, for a form is also provided in the *Book of Common Prayer,* is the church's prayer for healing. If we are to avoid picturing God in a strange way, we have to be careful about the theology surrounding this Sacrament. Its purpose is to reach deep within the recipient to free her or him to draw upon God's desire that we each may be whole. Certainly this includes the wholeness of the body, but it does not mean we ask God to go against his nature. The world was created finite and incomplete. It will remain that way and our physical selves must decay and die, even while the self may with God's power go from glory to glory.

I remember once being asked to pray for a young man who while rock climbing had fallen to a ledge some thirty feet down. I asked, "For what am I to pray?" I was told to pray that he might not be injured. The question that must be asked in turn was, "What would it look like if in the fall he had broken his leg and God now answered my prayer?" The Sacrament of Unction approaches the question differently. It asks that whatever may be the present physical condition of a person, that he or she be open to God's healing love in whatever form and to whatever end it may come. The focus is on the openness to God's presence.

The sacramental life implies a presence, which points to the third principle of Anglican pastoral care. This is that the church is an abiding, sacrificial presence to its people. The Anglican priest is sometimes referred to as the parson, which is derived from the word "person." It connotes an identifiable, personal presence within the community, which is both intimate and authentic.

We do not think that one can be an effective pastor to large numbers of people. Pastoring is not a matter of either celebrating the sacraments with congregations so vast that some cannot even see the face of the priest or of keeping office hours at which persons in trouble can talk to the priest for fifty minutes. In reading Herbert or in thinking of Deaconess Binns traveling on horseback through the mountains, it is clear that the Anglican pastoral idea is of the priest visiting the people where they live and work. There is no substitute for this and every member of an Anglican parish has the right to expect it.

Furthermore, Anglican priests seek to be living persons to their people, transparent and vulnerable. The priesthood is rooted in the receptive or left-handed mode of consciousness. Pastoral care is not fundamentally a profession, it is an art. It requires the priest letting people discover their own holiness in the broken and fallible witness of his or her own life. This process does not come to pass quickly, it requires faith and sacrifice. My experience is that it cannot be done without pain. The priest must carry the burden of countless projections laid upon him by those who he is called to serve. Such a burden becomes tolerable only when he or she has someone with whom that burden can be seen for what it is and shared. It is a cause for wonder in me how Deaconess Binns in her lonely service found a way to unburden herself of the load that she carried for the little community of Nora. Surely, she must have lived closely to our Lord.

The Anglican pastoral ideal is one of care from birth to death. In Herbert's day the parish priest was the civil registrar, who recorded the great events in a person's life, birth, marriage and death. Whereas this no longer is true, that curious vestige of a time now forever past, the parish register, remains a sign of the pastoral care of the person throughout life.

When an individual is born he or she is brought to the church to be baptized in the presence of the congregation at Sunday worship. So-called private baptisms are a contradiction of the symbolism of the sacrament. When that same person seeks the solemnization of his or her marriage they come to the church to receive God's blessing and to witness with their spouse to their intention. There is no more fitting place to make this witness before God and his people. "Tying the knot" at home plate, on the beach, or while skiing downhill is not only tacky, it trivializes marriage. When we die it is only right that our fellow Christians grieve our departure by offering the Eucharist in the presence of our body in the church. Anglicans are not buried from commercial funeral chapels, if they understand the nature of their faith.

To us the church building and the altar it shelters are witnesses to the nature of life; its redemption by Christ and our sacrifice which gives the daily routine its hope. For we believe that in our liturgy all space and all time is made whole by God's abiding presence. This is the rock upon which our pastoral intention is based.

Chapter Nine

Spirituality

Charles Moeller once observed that "the English spirit" is a "curious mixture of naive idealism and cynical empiricism." (cit. *Evelyn Underhill,* p.xx) This mixture has found its way into our religious outlook, with the strange result that we are particularly susceptible to enthusiasm, on the one hand, and are jaded on the other hand.

Enthusiasm is a common word for us all with a well known meaning; but it also has a technical meaning in theology. It comes from the Greek words *en theō,* "in God." What we associate with enthusiasm was originally symptomatic of one who was "in God." Consequently, enthusiasm in theology is the name given for persons who seek to find union with God as an ecstatic experience of one kind or another.

Enthusiasm takes one of two forms. The first, Pietism, is by far the most familiar in American religion. Pietism is the quest for the assurance of divine election in a felt experience of God called the "consolation." John Wesley wrote of his heart being "strangely warmed" after a meeting at Aldersgate. This was an experience of the consolation. Revivalism, which has swept across America time and time again from the 1740's to the present, operates on the expectations of Pietism. Billy Graham stands in a line of succession, beginning with Charles Finney and followed by Dwight Moody and Billy Sunday, of archevangelists who have preached for the experience of the consolation, the assurance of God's love for the sinner. Pietism can be best identified for its expectation of an immediate, identifiable, emotional payoff.

Pietism found its way into Anglicanism principally, although not exclusively, through John and Charles Wesley. It was the generating force in Evangelicalism, although one must avoid simplifications that distort. Pietism and the Puritan tradition are not identical and some Anglican Evangelicals are more Puritan or Reformed than Pietist. The Puritan tradition, it needs to be noted, is skeptical of the emotional experience of the consolation and looks for evidence of election as did Calvin in the fruits of one's daily life.

The other form of Enthusiasm is mysticism, which sees the union with God as the end of an ascent, requiring discipline, purgation, study, emptying and patience. Whereas classical Pietism dates from only the seventeenth century, mysticism is as old as Christianity and has always found fertile ground in Anglicanism. Our proclivity for thinking with the left hand gives to us a natural inclination for mysticism, which looks beyond the things visible to the invisible reality of God.

Mysticism is more at home in Anglican theology than Pietism. Reformed notions of election and consolation, which lie behind the Pietist expectation, are not congruent with the Anglican outlook. They lend themselves more to the juridical mind of Calvin than they do the inventiveness of a John Donne and a George Herbert. FitzSimons Allison in *The Rise of Moralism* has argued that beginning with Jeremy Taylor (1613-1667) the Anglican church departed from the pure doctrine of the Reformation and has pursued a spirituality which allows for mysticism. He regrets this and this is certainly his priviledge. My belief is that whether or not Taylor "is to blame," this point of view is in fact characteristic of the Anglican mind. I am well aware in saying this I am making a value judgement, but I think it is fair to our history and consonant with Christian truth.

Mysticism can easily be interpreted as a naive idealism, however. In the generation prior to World War I the English speaking peoples experienced a great interest in mysticism. William R. Inge (1860-1954), known as the "gloomy dean," gave the Bampton Lectures on *Christian Mysticism* (1899) and then wrote *Personal Idealism and Mysticism* (1907). Friedrich von Hugel (1852-1925), a widely read Roman Catholic scholar, wrote *The Mystical Element of Religion* (1908), a study in the writing of Catherine of Genoa and her associates. In this country William James (1842-1910) published *The Varieties of Religious Experience* (1902), which were actually the Gifford Lectures in Scotland. From our viewpoint today these books are dated. Yet they still provide rich insights. This is equally true of a book by Evelyn Underhill (1875-1941), entitled simply *Mysticism* (1911).

I have chosen Evelyn Underhill as the central figure for this chapter for a number of reasons. It is not because she is widely admired today. She is not. Martin Thornton, the author of *English Spirituality,* wrote of her in a highly derogatory fashion. There is no doubt she reflects a theology that is past, not to mention an England which died with World War II. She reveals in her own life a spiritual growth away from what is wrong in mysticism to what is right and healthy in the Anglican mystical tradition. She does this maintaining at the same time an ability to correct her idealism with her empiricism; which is to say that she developed a promising synthesis of the antithesis within the English spirit of naive idealism and cynical empiricism.

Evelyn Underhill was born in 1875 at the height of the Victorian era to a typical upper middle class English family. She was baptized and confirmed in the Church of England. She married at the age of thirty-two after many years of courtship, if one could call it a "courtship." Her husband was a solicitor. The impression is of a proper, if not passionless, relationship.

Underhill was always a writer. She began with fiction, in which the consistent theme was mysticism and incarnation. The first phase of her life's pilgrimage was from her maturity to 1906, during which time she considered herself an atheist. It is difficult to discover what she meant by atheism. In this period she, along with a number of English intellectuals, dabbled in the occult (e.g., witchcraft, communication with the dead, astrology, alchemy, etc.). Typical of her interests was an essay, "In Defense of Magic." The border line between psychic phenomena and the mystical experience has always been unclear.

Charles Williams (1886-1945), one of the Inklings mentioned before, was a younger friend of Underhill and shared her interests in the occult and the hermetical literature (i.e., ancient occult writings attributed to Hermes Trismegistus). Williams later drew on this material to write in defense of Christianity in hope of appealing to English speaking intellectuals who were steeped in this tradition of psychic phenomena. Among those same intellectuals were C. S. Lewis (1898-1963) and T. S. Eliot (1888-1965).

Underhill and Williams crossed the border between the occult and mysticism going in a Christian direction. It is not uncommon for Anglicans to pass the opposite direction. For example, James Pike (1913-1969), sometime Bishop of California, spent the last months of his life using mediums to make contact with his son, who had committed suicide. I knew Pike as a man with a very bright theological mind, given to eccentric notions. Societies for the study of spiritualism inevitably carry among their boards the names of Anglican priests. England has more ghosts running around in it than any other land, with the possible exception of North America to which this interest was brought by our English forebearers. We might remember also the horrors of the Salem witch trials in Massachusetts among good English stock. The occult is the dark side of mysticism and thinking with the left hand.

When Underhill began to consider herself a theist it was not as an Anglican theist. She had a great deal of disdain for the Church of England, and properly so. The Edwardian Church of England was not very lively — more cynically empirical than naively idealistic. This was equally true, incidently, of Anglicanism in this country. Underhill's religious faith was a matter of individual devotion coupled with an ongoing flirtation with the more creative edge of Roman Catholicism. She found, on the other hand, the Pronouncements of Pius X (1835-1914) against Modernism offensive to her basic empirical approach. (Modernism accepted biblical criticism, contemporary philosophy and interpreted history in terms of its goals, all ideas which are commonplace today.) Underhill's husband, who possessed a certain "English common sense," also restrained Underhill's more romantic ideas of Rome. Consequently, she attended the Eucharist in Roman churches, counseled with Roman Catholic priests and wrote on mysticism.

Her book, *Mysticism,* is one of her two major works. It is indicative of an individualist piety, which is both romantic and empirical. Underhill's definition of mysticism is generic (i.e., a conclusion drawn from speculative theology), which is a pre-eminently Anglican outlook. This means that every person has the capacity for mystical experience, which is why I have in this chapter viewed mysticism as the logical end of the spiritual life. Mysticism also expresses Underhill's own bias against the institutional church. She was pursuing her own, individual pilgrimage.

This individualism is common in Anglican spirituality. It is an improvement over the fascination with the occult, but the individual quest reflects an eccentricity and, perhaps, naivete. Its contemporary expression is exemplified when an interest in Jungian psychology among Anglicans becomes inordinate. Analytical psychology is an individualistic psychology, largely based on dream interpretation and free association with a danger of becoming agnostic. As one who personally has found the pilgrimage of Carl Jung (1875-1961) immensely illuminating, I do not wish to be misunderstood. I am criticizing the reduction of a very large metaphor to an analytical system, in order to make it respectable to be a "Jungian" in our unimaginative world.

A friend of mine was getting his doctorate in religion and personality under a Baptist professor. On one occasion, he mentioned that he was in analysis with a Jungian. The response his professor made in disgust was, "Don't become one of those flakey Episcopalians." There is some truth in the admonition. The inner journey, the flight of the one to the One, the soul stripped naked before God, and such are all included to render one "flakey," whether it is done in the name of Jung or Meister Eckhart (1260-1328), if it is not tempered by a commitment to the church. It renders us susceptible to many valid criticisms of mysticism, the chief among which is that it can be a far cry from the Christian Gospel.

About 1920, the anti-institutionalism in Underhill passed and she returned at age forty-five to the church of her childhood. This began the third and most healthy phase of her pilgrimage. Why she did this is not certain, but von Hügel was a strong influence. Once active in the Church of England Underhill became a spiritual director for countless priests. Her retreats were famous. She was an active, though conservative presence in the fourth movement of the Catholic revival. Her teaching was always a bit too cozy — she was the Agatha Christie of spirituality — and her theology smacks of seventeenth century French piety, but she was able to reconcile a lifetime of searching to Anglicanism and to make a positive difference. Her second major work, *Worship* (1936), was very much in the spirit of the "Parish and People" movement of A. G. Hebert and reveals a spirituality grounded in the church and her liturgy.

The qualities of a healthy Anglican spirituality, to which Underhill's life and work point in many ways, begins with the empirical base. We believe that the common experience of humanity has transcendental implications. Four aspects of such a spirituality come to mind. Whereas I would not claim that Underhill would agree with me entirely, I think that they are implied in her work.

First, Anglican spirituality is earthy. I have little doubt that a Victorian like Underhill, well-trained in that ancient rabbinic saying which became watchword of nineteenth century Christianity, "Cleanliness is next to godliness," would not agree with this as boldly stated. Underhill's Anglican contemporary, William Temple, did tell us that Christianity is the most materialistic of all world religions and Underhill herself wrote in *Mysticism,* "Sacraments, too, however simple their beginnings, always tend, as they evolve, to assume upon the phenomenal plane a magical aspect" (p. 163). What she may not have seen was that this is because the sacraments are rooted in the earth in all its chthonic power. ("Chthonic" has no synonym. It calls for a receptive consciousness and describes the underworld of ancient mythology, with all its fearsome energy.)

In the anthropological studies of Judaism it is considered probable that the dietary laws protect people from chaos, which is present in an earthiness. Hebrew religion had a great fear of chaos, which is why the sea, for example, was considered so terrible. Northern European religions on the other hand, were willing to divinize the powers of the darkness and drew on their energy for the creative spirit from them. Woden/Wotan/Odin, from whom we get "Wednesday," was the god of war, poetry, knowledge and wisdom — an interesting constellation of experience rooted in left hand thinking. This element was not lost, even when it was suppressed, in northern European Christianity, including Anglicanism.

One commonplace access to the chthonic powers of the earth is obscenity. It literally means what does not fit. A trivialization of the obscene is the dirty joke, whose humor is built on the incongruous and is the obverse of our fear of the dark mysteries of life associated, particularly, with the orifices of the body. With all its love for decency and order, perhaps because of it, there is sometimes an irrepressible delight in Anglicanism for the obscene. Is it possible that obscenity taps an energy for mystical union? Is this why DuBose suggests we speak kindly of Satan? Is it possible that magic is a perversion of our awareness of powers of the earth?

Secondly, Anglican spirituality grows out of liturgical prayer, out of the sacraments rooted in the earth. The image that comes to my mind is a storm on a lake whose waters are deep. As we know, a storm on a shallow lake is far more dangerous than one where there is a stability borne of the depths. Anglican piety emerges from a life steeped in the *Book of Common Prayer*. This means that it is perhaps not as dramatic or showy as some might wish, but it has a persistence, a rootedness, and a perspective which endures. Its piety might be described as pre-eminently orthodox, understanding "orthodox" in its root meaning of straight or true.

Spirituality that emerges from liturgical prayer has a fecundity of imagery and an assurance that comes from a long acquaintance with the tradition. Too much that passes for piety is thin and cloying. Public prayers and spiritual songs preach at us and presume to tell God the latest events. Anglican spirituality, when it is true to itself, is deeper than the cultural expectations and the WASP Jesus of the Moral Majority of the 1980 presidential campaign. It is our life in the sacraments that frees us from the impoverishment of popular religion.

Thirdly, Anglican spirituality draws on a biblical imagery. The traditional form of Anglican spiritual direction has been "biblical admonition." There is no "spirituality of the Bible" anymore than there is a "theology of the Bible." Scriptures reach across many cultural expressions of piety, just as there are multiple theological efforts in the Scriptures to understand the experience of God. The Bible is a source of enrichment to the symbolic world of the person at prayer. The Scriptures are the poetry of the Christian, and Anglicanism is very much content to let them be that without efforts to control the outcome.

When we read the great Christian spiritual masters through the ages — e.g., Origen (185-254), Gregory of Nyssa (c. 330-c. 395) Bernard of Clairvaux (1090-1153), Saint Bonaventure (1221-1274), Johannes Tauler (1300-1361), John Woolman (1720-1772), Theophan the Recluse (1815-1894) — each has their distinct outlook and each reveals to us something new in Christ's illumination of our lives. They all are steeped in the Scriptures and quote them again and again. It is obvious they were fed by reading Holy Writ and yet that reading only opened their eyes and stimulated their imaginations to see God as he had not been seen before. This is the Anglican understanding of the Bible as a source for spiritual growth.

Fourthly, Anglican spirituality is collaborative. This means that there is a tension between collective truth and individual insight. We do not wish to quench the spirit and the only typical Anglican is a typical Anglican. We are a collection of individuals. Yet in our better moments we know that we need to examine our own peculiar prilgrimage against the church's quest for two thousand years. If this works there is an accumulation of wisdom which enriches us all. This requires us to be both secure in our own prayer life and open to the offerings of the past and those around us.

This tension creates a certain dis-ease. It is to our benefit that the dis-ease leaves us vulnerable to the transcendent world. It cuts through the Pharisee in us all and reveals our own fundamental spiritual impoverishment and need for grace. We must be uncomfortable with our own dis-ease, not proud of it.

In *The School of Charity* Evelyn Underhill quoted Joseph Cardinal Mercier (1851-1926), who said that we are added to the church not just for the sake of our souls, but "in order to extend the Kingdom of Love." Ignatius Loyola (1491-1556) describes this love. He wrote that contemplation seeks to attain the love of God and "that love ought to manifest itself in deeds rather than words," and "that love consists in the mutual sharing of goods." This is not a quality of Anglican spirituality anymore than it is a tenent of Communism; it is the test of an authentic spirituality. The last three chapters will be devoted to describing the Anglican response to this test.

Chapter Ten

Mission

During World War II Allied pilots shot down over the Melansian Islands were terrified to find themselves falling into the hands of the natives, who were often most frightening in appearance. The natives' hair particularly was dressed in what we would now call a large Afro, a round, bushy mass. The downed pilots discovered to their amazement that these savage looking men treated them with great gentleness, hiding them from the Japanese and tending their wounds. The natives of Melanesia came to be called "fuzzy-wuzzy angels." They were Christians and the assumption they made was that those fighting the Japanese were Christians as well.

The Christians of Melanesia are a living memorial to John Coleridge Patteson (1827-1871), the first Bishop of Melanesia. Patteson was the embodiment of the unpretentious, quiet missionary, whose sacrifice in the cause of Christ goes almost unnoticed because of our proclivity to the understatement. Patteson was born into the English upper class. His great uncle was Samuel Taylor Coleridge (1772-1834), known to almost every school boy and girl as a poet, but more important he was a creative fundamental theologian who needs to be rediscovered. Patteson's father was a judge. He sent his son to all the best schools.

In 1841 at the age of fourteen, young Patteson met and heard George Augustus Selwyn (1809-1878) preach, who had just been appointed the first missionary bishop to New Zealand. Selwyn, who was a friend of the family, was influenced by the Tractarians, as Patteson came to be. Patteson was deeply impressed by Selwyn's sermon, which spoke of going out to establish a new church, to die neglected and forgotten. That turned out to be more prophetic of Patteson than it did Selwyn himself. Having studied at Oxford, Patteson was ordained Deacon in 1853 and left for New Zealand to assist Selwyn in the church's outreach to the Melanesian Islands. There has always been something familiar about Anglican styles. Our lives are lived closely together and often what one does depends on whom he or she knows.

It is hard for us to realize the nature of Patteson's decision. He had no reason to think that having once left England he would ever see his family again. No doubt that at age twenty-six he was filled with the romance of the adventure, but he was going to the other side of the world to serve a strange people. The voyage alone was a long ordeal. His published correspondence to family and friends reveals a man devoted to his home, and yet committed to bringing the message of Christ to the people of the South Pacific.

The missionary method of Selwyn and Patteson was to reach out to the young people and to establish schools where they could be educated. Patteson began this in Auckland, New Zealand, but quickly moved north to the Loyalty Islands. It is interesting to read of his visit to Pitcairn Island, where the mutineers from the *Bounty* had settled in 1790. Patteson's love for his students and his ability to reach them was remarkable. This passage from a letter back home, written after he had become bishop, is indicative of his commitment. Dysentery had struck the school. He wrote,

I write from the dining hall (now our hospital), with eleven Melanesians lying around me in extremity of peril. I buried two today in one grave, and I baptized another now dying by my side. . . .

When I buried those two children today, my heart was full, I durst not think, but could only pray and believe and trust in Him.

The Melanesian Islands are the home of a great variety of people, speaking many languages. In 1856, private friends gave Patteson a boat to travel those islands. It was called "The Southern Cross," as each of the successive boats of the Bishop of Melanesia has been called. Patteson taught himself to communicate in thirty different languages, and was fluent in five or six. This was the heart of his mission to these people. They knew him as a friend, who represented a Christian community that cared.

He was ordained Bishop of Melanesia in 1861 by the bishops of New Zealand. At first he moved back and forth on the Southern Cross between New Zealand and the Melanesian Islands. This became too difficult and in 1864, he settled on Norfolk Island. His home became a center for the training of young clergy and his sensitive pastoral work.

In 1868, Selwyn had returned to England after twenty-seven years, to become Bishop of Lichfield, but Patteson remained on. In 1871, he went on a tour of a number of islands. While becalmed off Nukapu he wrote Selwyn at Lichfield,

> And now what will the next few days bring forth? It may be God's will that the opening for the Gospel may be given to us now. Sometimes I feel as if I were too importunate in my longing for some beginning here; and I try not to be impatient, and to wait his good time, knowing that it will come when it is the fulness of time.

The next day, September 20, he went ashore on Nukapu with several companions. He never returned alive. Patteson was killed, his head crushed with a war club. Several of his companions died later from poisoned arrows. Patteson was killed not because he represented Christ, but in revenge for five men who had been kidnapped by a labor party from Fiji. He was a victim of human greed, anger and ignorance.

Patteson's last recorded words were written to the man who thirty years before had invited him to be a missionary and to die in a lonely place. They were full of the faith that God in his time would make the good news known in that place, as throughout the world. When we remember him and his companions in the church year every September 20, it would behoove us to think what was in this young man's life in the Church of England that called him to a watery martyr's grave. It was not the idea of making Englishmen of the Melanesians, but opening them to the freedom that is in Christ. As our pilots discovered seventy years later, "the blood of the martyrs is the seed of the church."

Patteson stands in a long tradition of Anglican missionaries. Ireland was converted by the British Patrick (389-461) — a fact which the Irish are not at pains to broadcast. Willibrord (658-739) preached to the Frisians in what is now the Netherlands. Boniface (680-754) evangelized Germany and died a martyr. After the Reformation, the outreach of the Church of England took two forms: what is quaintly called "the church of the British dispersion" and the work of the missionary societies.

The British are a traveling people. Consequently, in 1634 the Bishop of London was given jurisdiction over English congregations overseas. As we have already noted, due to the failure to provide bishops for the church abroad the growth of Anglicanism was greatly hampered. The church of the British dispersion did, however, reach to North America, India, Australia and, as we have seen, to New Zealand. By the nineteenth century, bishops were provided.

The work of the missionary societies supplemented and even more augmented the missionary outreach of the Church of England. It needs to be remembered that these societies are independent from the hierarchy. The first was the Society for Promoting Christian Knowledge (SPCK) in 1698 and then the Society for the Propagation of the Gospel (SPG) in 1701. These two societies did a noble work in North America at great human cost. It is estimated that 25 percent of the priests whom they sent to North America died on the voyage over — unknown witnesses to Christ whom we should hold in honor.

In 1799, the Evangelical party founded the Church Missionary Society (CMS) and ten years later the Church Mission to Jews (CMJ) was started. The CMS spear-headed the mission of the Church of England in the nineteenth century. In 1844, the South American Missionary Society (SAMS) was started. Like the CMS it is strongly Evangelical. The Catholic revival developed its missionary outreach around the Melanesian Mission, founded in 1849, and the University Mission to Central Africa, (UMCA), begun in 1858. John Keble was active in the Melanesian Mission and was instrumental in providing Patteson with the second Southern Cross. David Livingstone (1813-1873) — of "Dr. Livingstone I presume" fame (the purported first words of H. M. Stanley of the New York *Herald* upon finding him exhausted in the remote wilds of Africa) — was associated with the UMCA in 1861. A Congregationalist working for Anglican missions, Livingstone is best known as an explorer.

There were still other missionary societies in the Church of England after this. One that deserves mention if for no other reason than it seems a little incredible is the Bible Christians Missionary Society (BCMS) which in 1922 broke off from the CMS because the latter was too liberal. The UCMA has more recently joined with the SPG to form the USPG, which now represents the missionary outreach of the more Catholic-minded in the Church of England.

The Episcopal Church wisely did not create independent missionary societies and it did not intentionally base its missionary outreach on churchmanship. Instead, it made the entire church a missionary society. In 1837, the Domestic and Foreign Missionary Society was created and this remains today the corporate title of the national church. The first missionary sent overseas by this society went to Persia where a small but very courageous Anglican church survives, even though it is now outlawed. Some of these Persian Christians have been added to the list of the martyrs since the establishment of the Islamic republic there in 1979.

Perhaps, most notable of the work of the Domestic and Foreign Missionary Society was among the native Americans. There are three counties in the United States where the majority of the people are Episcopalians: two in South Dakota and one in Wyoming. All three counties encompass Indian reservations.

There is no doubt that missionary enthusiasm among Anglicans waxes and wanes. Often when we are preoccupied with our own internal problems we lose interest, much to the distress of those representing us around the world. Yet we need to keep in mind that there are approximately sixty-five million Anglicans, of whom at least 40 percent are non-Caucasian! Less than half of the Anglicans in the world live in England. Most notable has been the growth of Anglicanism in Africa.

What often confuses the observer is that they look at Anglican missionary efforts out of a theology of mission which is not typical of Anglicanism. It is important to reflect on someone such as John Coleridge Patteson and discern the presuppositions of Anglican missionary theology. I list three.

First, mission is the activity of the church as church, not a loose confederation of individuals formed into a society. One of the great problems presented by various Evangelical missionary societies (CMS, SAMS, BCMS) is their failure to understand this. It is the purpose of the church's mission to plant and nurture the church in another land and then to let it be the church of those people. Patteson moved quickly to train Melanesians as priests. Practically all the bishops in that province are now Melanesian. Far too often in the past Christians in the "third" and "fourth world" feel patronized and diminished by arrogant Anglican missionaries who treat them as incapable of managing their own lives.

This means that our task is not to send out a person who will provoke a "conversion experience" in other individuals. Obviously, we seek conversion — but conversion to an understanding of a people's life and culture as fulfilled in Christ. Christ must be discovered incarnate in them. This can most readily be observed in the liturgical life of their church, which most needs draw from their culture's symbolic world and not that of England or America. The Anglican cathedral in Nairobi could just as well be standing in Salisbury or York. It is embarrassing to contrast it with the Roman Catholic cathedral in that same city, which is African to the core.

Once when I was in Nairobi, a "European" (as we are called) remarked "how ugly" he thought the Roman Catholic cathedral. This is beside the point. Our taste is not to be considered.

In 1963, the Anglican Communion adopted a missionary policy of mutual sharing. In 1973, this was given a methodology in what is called "partners in mission." It is our belief that every province of the Anglican Communion has gifts for every other province that need to be shared. Behind this approach is the commitment to a theology of mission as church. I have developed this theology at some greater length in a book entitled *Turning to Christ* (Seabury, 1981). Here the distinction between a revivalist approach, perhaps more characteristic of the Church Growth movement in the United States and the Anglican approach, simply needs to be identified.

Secondly, Anglicanism believes in mission by identification and participation. One lives with the people, identifies with their culture, and participates to the degree that it is emotionally possible. No one can become another culture; but neither do we make our own social context the condition for being in Christ. The symbol of the mission compound, where we once lived as if it were Canterbury or Washington, is what we must overcome if we are really serious about separating "white man's burden" from the Gospel.

What is it we bring? Why go? We bring a commitment to knowledge, but that comes under the next point. We also bring commitment to the Christ who transcends and transforms culture. At the heart of the Gospel is the belief that in Christ we discover that in dying we find new life. The Passion, the death and resurrection, is a universal, transcultural symbol of a life free from the fear of death, which fear gives injustice, oppression and poverty its power. Our witness to the world is that God is loving, personal and present, as declared in the Incarnation of his Son. It is his world and not the world of Satan. This is what we bring and very little more.

We are told in the account of Patteson's death that it was his custom to move from his small boat to the native canoe, that he might be paddled to shore by the local inhabitants. This was for him a symbol of his trust in them and their ways. He believed that his trust would provoke trust of him and his motives. There is an obvious risk here, realized in Patteson's own death. It is an image of what it means to do a mission as one who identifies and participates with those to whom he or she is sent.

Thirdly, Anglicanism believes that mission must be education. It is not our purpose to make people more guilty. As Vincent Donovan, a Roman Catholic missionary in East Africa, has pointed out, whether it is expressed as we recognize it or not, people are already guilty. It is our privilege to help them to become aware of forgiveness. We are convinced that as people become more conscious of themselves and their world that they become more open to the Gospel. Christ reveals to us the truth and it is the truth that makes us free. Even for the non-Christian there is a continuity between what he knows naturally and what God reveals to us.

This is as true in our local community as it is for a mission to the other side of the world. We do not censure the media, because we believe that the truth has its own authenticity that will prevail. We do not ridicule the values others hold most dear, because we believe that God is never without his witnesses. We do not demand conformity to one set of ideas, because we believe that there is always more to be known. We do not deny people access to information, because we believe if people truly seek to know they will be ultimately led to God.

Patteson developed his mission to Melanesia around education. He was martyred out of ignorance. It is learning that becomes the medium of grace and overcomes our fears. The place for today's missionary is in the school, in the government, in the industry, on the farms, where our skills become a witness to the Lord who was among us as a carpenter.

The word mission means "sending." God is one who sends. He sends his Son and he sends his Holy Spirit. He sends us as well. There is no question that the church is called to be as one sent into the world, as well as to herself. Sending is not of one kind and it is not necessarily done in the way that the culture most commonly conceives of what it means to be in mission. Anglicanism believes that it is sent. How else would a Christian consciousness peculiar to a people on a few moderate size islands in the North Atlantic now surround the globe? It is not enough just to go into the world; we have to go thoughtfully, believing in a God who sent his reason into the world that the darkness, even the darkness of the blindly enthusiastic, might not overcome the world.

Chapter Eleven

Church and State

For many people the church loses its credibility when it makes common cause with the state. When the Roman Emperor Constantine (288-337) recognized Christianity for various and complex reasons somehow the purity went out of our witness. The presumption of Henry VIII in declaring himself head of the Church in England is in this same despised tradition of caesaropapism. We see a similar arrangement today in Russia, where the Orthodox church is little more than a department of the state, a situation which began, incidently, long before the Soviets.

The institutions of the Church of England, as I have already indicated, are more appropriately traced to Elizabeth I than her father, and she never declared herself the head of the Church in England. At the same time, because the Church of England is the established church in that land, it has always been subject to the charge of Erastianism: the belief that the state is supreme to the church in ecclesiastical matters. Occasionally this is a valid charge. Richard Hooker, for example, was an Erastian. This suspicion has colored common expectations of Anglicanism's attitude toward the state. To some people we put a high premium upon sanctifying what the state wishes to do and are weak in our witness against evil in high places.

Although our hands are not always clean, Erastianism is not characteristic of us. Going far back in our history, Dunstan (c. 909-988) was a figure in Anglo-Saxon politics, earning the wrath of some kings and the support of others in his reform of the church. Far better known is Thomas Becket (1118-1170), who defended the church against the state in the person of Henry II and as a result died a martyr. Thomas More (1478-1535), who was martyred for refusing to accept the Act of Supremacy of Henry VIII, is more typical of the Anglican spirit than he is a traitor to the English throne. We do not have to agree with the issue at hand to celebrate the conviction that leads to a decision to oppose the state at personal risk. Such a figure is the first bishop of Louisiana, Leonidas Polk (1806-1864), who died for his convictions as a Confederate general at the Battle of Pine Mountain.

Freshest in our memory is the quiet witness of the martyred Archbishop of Uganda, Janani Luwum (1922-1977). In many ways Luwum was a typical African Anglican. A member of the Acholi tribe from northern Uganda, Luwum was the son of a church teacher. After an experience of conversion in 1948, he studied first to become a lay reader and then to become a priest at Buwalasi Theological College. He was ordained in 1956 and shortly thereafter spent a year in study in England. After parish work he went back to Buwalasi on the staff. Following three more years of study in England, he returned to become Principal of Buwalasi, only to see it merged with Bishop Tucker Theological College in 1966.

There was nothing particularly unusual about this. Buwalasi was not a very good college and Luwum was probably fortunate to be relieved of his post there. He became provincial secretary in Uganda briefly and then in 1967 was elected Bishop of Northern Uganda. History began to close in on Luwum. At heart he was a skilled pastor, who cared for his priests and their families. My principal informant as to the life of Luwum was his young protégé, Emmanuel Twesigye, who was even counseled by him as to the choice of an appropriate wife for a priest. He was not to complete his ministry as a pastor. God called him to a different witness.

Uganda, a beautiful land, is tragically divided by tribalism and Christian-Muslim strife. A new constitution under Dr. Milton Obote had created in 1966 a diocese for the Archbishop of Uganda. Previously, the Archbishop ran things from whatever was his original diocese. Logically located at the capital of Kampala, the archepiscopal diocese was carved out of the Diocese of Namirembe, which is populated by the Baganda tribe. The Baganda were very unhappy about this diminishment of their diocese and threatened to form their own province. In 1974, Luwum became Archbishop and had to solve this festering problem. Ironically enough, he had the assistance of Idi Amin, a Muslim who had overthrown Obote and was now President of Uganda. I can recall being told of the cordial, working relationship between Luwum and Amin at this time. As a result, the Baganda stayed within the Province of Uganda.

In 1975 for reasons of his own, Amin began to persecute the Christian church, murdering its people and driving them out of the army. Members of certain tribes were systematically exterminated. It was a classic ploy to maintain power by creating a supposed enemy to the state requiring extraordinary action. For a long time, Luwum was privately aware of the danger of Amin, but it was only when genocide and persecution of the Christians became apparent that he spoke out against his regime.

Amin lumped the church leadership with those who sought to overthrow him and on December 26, 1976, he charged the bishops with inciting treason in their Christmas sermons. The secret police was turned loose on the church leadership. The Archbishop's house was searched and nothing found. A bishop was arrested and church people disappeared. Luwum tried to see Amin to no avail. He could not reach him by phone. So on February 10, 1976, the bishops of Uganda under Luwum's leadership felt compelled by the Gospel to write a memorandum condemning the evils of Amin's rule.

This was too much for Amin and he searched the Archbishop's house once again and claimed to have found a cache of weapons. On February 16, 1977, Amin called leaders of the armed forces and the church to a viewing at the public square of these weapons (which were obviously Amin's own Soviet arms) and to hear letters purportedly written by Obote to Luwum, calling for the overthrow of Amin. Luwum went to this meeting, despite warnings to flee, saying, "In all this we must seek the hand of God." The army shouted for Luwum's death in a manner reminiscent of our Lord's Passion. Luwum and two cabinet ministers were murdered shortly afterwards. The report was that Amin himself shot Luwum in the mouth for defiance and then he was shot in the chest and the back as he fell, a martyr to Christ.

At this writing, the grave of Janani Luwum at his cathedral in Namirembe lies empty, awaiting the return of his body from where Amin buried it in northern Uganda. Although God did not, as some in Uganda thought he would, strike Amin dead for this great blasphemy, the martyrdom of Luwum galvanized the resistance to Amin and he was overthrown. When Amin dies he will be happily forgotten, and it will be Janani Luwum and his gentle witness as a pastor turned martyr which will be honored by Ugandans and church people everywhere.

Archbishop Luwum's life illustrates what is a basic Anglican conviction. We do in fact believe that government is an instrument of God's purpose, imperfect as it undoubtedly is. In fact the state has a responsibility for establishing a climate where the Spirit may do its work among the people. This was seen in Luwum's willingness to work with the Muslim leader, Idi Amin, to resolve the Bagandan crisis in the Anglican church in Uganda. In turn, Luwum gave his allegiance to the government. He sought to work for a better Uganda for all.

Any notion of the separation of church and state, however, implies that Christian commitment is only a matter of private conscience and that the political realm is not our concern as Christians and is alien to Anglican thinking. The memorandum of the Ugandan bishops was completely appropriate. The kings and queens of England are consecrated by the church and are by that act beholden to the church as an instrument of God's purpose. The responsibility of rulers to God and his church that lies behind the Church's consecration of the English monarchs is probably more central to Anglicanism even today than what was in the mind of the eighteenth century framers of the United States Constitution, who sought to divorce the ecclesiastical hierarchy from the influence over government.

It is helpful here to reflect briefly upon Ernst Troeltsch's (1865-1923) classic distinction between the church and sect typologies of religion. A church typology is typical of those expressions of Christianity that are inclusive, related to the state, and in which people are members by virtue of birth. A sect typology is characteristic of exclusive Christian interpretations, alien to the state, which recruit their members by means of conversion. By the late eighteenth century, American religion was increasingly characterized by a sect typology, which in fact created a religious climate supportive of the Revolution. Anglicanism is typical of a church typology. Consequently, there has never been a good fit between our understanding of the relationship of church and state and the interpretation of the Constitution which would encourage a dichotomy between public political affairs and private religion.

We believe that God can use politics for his own ends. Anglicanism does not think that being a politician is an unworthy calling or that the political process is necessarily corrupt. Even if it is, the Spirit can move through broken human institutions just as it does through sinful individuals like ourselves. Well-meaning efforts to avoid political advocacy inevitably end up turning over the power to change things to people who are neither scrupulous nor guided by a desire to know and do God's will. Be it in the church or any other institution, an intelligent and discerning employment of political power is a responsibility laid upon us.

In this light, Anglicanism traditionally has a much higher percentage of the elected officials in the United States government than would be expected based on our percentage of the population as a whole. The subtle symbolism of St. John's Church across Lafayette Square from the White House and the National Cathedral of St. Peter and St. Paul occupying the highest point in the District of Columbia has a certain clout. There are historical and sociological reasons for this. It confers on us a particular responsibility which for all its abstruseness should not be ignored out of embarrassment or a fear of triumphalism.

The assumption is that the church, any church, is charged with speaking on behalf of the Gospel to the government. In other words, there is an obedience to which Christians are called that is higher than the law of the state. Anglicanism understands that in the face of obvious, overt, political evil, when all legal means for redress are blocked to us and after careful thought civil disobedience is not only appropriate for Christians, but required. This may even include the overthrow of an evil ruler. This came to be the intention of the church in Uganda and it was a morally commendable act. The most effective way of doing this action was, tragically enough, through the martyrdom of its archbishop.

In the U.S. presidential election of 1980, much criticism was leveled at the so-called Moral Majority, which actively campaigned for and against candidates on the basis of their record in support of principles held by the membership of this movement. There was nothing wrong from an Anglican viewpoint in the principle of voting on the basis of one's religious convictions, even where it is a collective, organized campaign. In fact, we all should vote our religious conscience. The criticism of the Moral Majority from the viewpoint of Anglicanism is substantive. The Moral Majority, which stands in the sectarian, revivalist tradition of American religion understands Christian morality in a very different way than does Anglicanism. We do not believe, for example, that ethical questions are reducible to black and white norms of conduct, as in the matter of abortion. Any effort to push an absolutist approach violates our commitment to encouraging responsible, reasonable, free choice. This is reason enough to oppose the moralism of the Moral Majority, which is in the spirit of prohibition and oppressive laws such as the banning of the sale of contraceptives and defining sodomy.

Sometimes the Anglican rejection of sectarian passion and moral righteousness leaves the impression we are the church of the upper classes, who substitute aesthetics for religious fervor and call it a reasonable faith. Some years ago, a popular analysis of American upward social mobility came out with a chapter on religion entitled "From Pentecostal to Episcopal." The implication was that at the top of the social ladder lay membership in the Episcopal church. There may be some truth in that. It used to be said that everyone in New York City was either Jewish, Roman Catholic, agnostic or Episcopalian, implying that if you did not come from an ethnic religious group, the only options for the sophisticated people of our greatest city were either unbelief or Episcopalianism. Whatever truth there may have been in this quip, the prestige of being an Episcopalian and its value for success is, thank God, diminishing.

The evidence is, however, that neither the Episcopal church in particular nor Anglicanism in general has a demographic profile favoring the upper socio-economic classes. I have already mentioned that the three counties in the United States where the majority of people are Episcopalians all encompass Indian reservations. Even those parishes which have a reputation for being "fashionable" have their share of poor folk on the rolls. It is inaccurate to speak of us as simply the church of the privileged. The Africa of Janani Luwum is a poverty stricken third world, where millions of Anglicans worship in stark simplicity.

What in fact may create the impression of our being an upper class church is a lingering establishment mentality even in the third world, which comes across as snobbery. I remember once having dinner with an African archbishop. It was as formal as if we were eating in Buckingham Palace. The one concession to contemporary outlook was that a woman in our party was permitted to join us for dinner. I had been briefed beforehand on what topics of conversation were permitted and what I could not say. It was an incredible experience.

[There is someone with whom I very much desire a close relationship, who is a clergyman in another denomination. He loathes the Anglican church, and I sense an unsurmountable barrier between us. As much as either of us may want to climb over it, a century's old inheritance of an association with an Anglicanism of a stuffy English peerage, arrogant American millionaires and the confusion of ideology with the Gospel makes it very difficult. It may be that we have not yet awakened to the fact that Anglicanism is disestablished everywhere save in England.]

It is because of this persistent image of privilege, coupled with an ecclesial noblesse oblige, that other Christians sometimes find it difficult to take our ecumenical rhetoric seriously. Anglicans are committed, for example, to the Lund principle, which is that we will not do separately what we can do together. It sounds wonderful, but I know of very little decision making in the Episcopal church done on that principle. Consequently, what comes across to others is that we can do whatever is being done better by virtue of the fact that we are doing it and consequently we go our separate way.

What makes Anglican pride even that much more infuriating to others is that we reveal so little in which to boast. We often play it safe theologically, ethically and liturgically by adhering to a pendantic principle of moderation and good taste which obscures our commitment to Christ. A charge often leveled at us is that we lack a theology. This is not true, but it is often difficult to name one Anglican theologian who has made much difference outside the Anglican Communion.

Yet in spite of this seemingly calculated tepidity, Anglicanism produces its heroes. We do not possess the kind of systematic mind, which creates a theology that endures the ages. Our saints are usually of a different kind than Aquinas, Luther or Calvin. Sometimes we witness in spite of our theology. Certainly, there is not much in the kind of heavyhanded Pietism imported to Africa by the Church Missionary Society that would inspire one to withstand Idi Amin, and yet Luwum knew the Gospel and what it requires of us; namely, that we be faithful.

Like Luwum, we are at our best when we love the Lord and his church more than we love our style of life. We do not believe in our country, right or wrong. If evil has such a grip upon the institutions of government, we know that evil must be overthrown by one means or another. We are not monarchists, republicans or socialists, although our membership includes them all and more. We are pilgrims, who want to pass through a land that will support our journey to the Kingdom; and, if need be, the noblest of us will choose to occupy that land for a bit shorter time than usual rather than deny the Lord of the Kingdom.

Chapter Twelve

Prophetic Witness

One thing which I would hope has struck the reader by now is the infinite variety of people that make up the Anglican Communion. Two things seem to follow from this. The first is that everyone does not have to be an example of everything. In other words, John Coleridge Patteson may embody our spirit of mission, but he does not have to also possess the spiritual insights of a Julian of Norwich, who apparently never left that small English town. This can be justified by the second observation. In our common life of worship, which is what cements Anglicans together, we can affirm the different gifts of one another without having to live as if they were ours as well. In our understanding of the church, it is the people of God who provide a comprehensive ministry, not each individual.

As we come to this concluding chapter it is particularly important to make this point. Not everyone is called to die at the hands of Idi Amin, to revise the liturgy or to translate the Scriptures. But we all are called to serve in a community where these things are possible and where we support the vocation of anyone who has a God-given gift to make a singular contribution in a given area even when it impinges upon our own comfort. We should not do this uncritically, but we need to be clear about the principle. This is particularly true in the matter of prophetic witness.

There is no doubt that the biblical concept of the Kingdom calls for a ministry to the suffering, the imprisoned, the oppressed, the hungry and whomever is dehumanized by an unjust society. In the abstract, almost all of us can affirm this with enthusiasm. When it is the vocation, however, of one of our number to make this Gospel imperative a matter demanding our specific attention and requiring us to change our comfortable ways, then many of us fall away. The prophet has never been popular among his other contemporaries. He has been stoned, beheaded, crucified and shot. If not killed, we have been all too ready to vilify him or her in the name of God, little realizing that it may well be God who sent the prophet to challenge our complacency.

The Anglican Communion has been blessed with its prophets. William Wilberforce (1759-1833), a devout Evangelical and member of Parliament, toiled for years to achieve the abolishment of the English slave trade. It was accomplished just before his death. William Augustus Muhlenberg (1796-1877), rector of the Church of the Holy Communion, built the first parish house in the Episcopal church as a base to do work among the poor and neglected of New York City. Henry Scott Holland (1874-1918), a theologian and preacher, was the brilliant spokesman for the Christian Social Union, which sought to apply, in the face of *laissez faire* economics, the principles of the Gospel to the plight of England's workers. These three persons are representative of a list that could go on and on.

It is my conviction that when the history of the Episcopal church in the twentieth century is written the name of one of its great prophets will be John E. Hines (born 1910), the twenty-second Presiding Bishop, a man so controversial that he had, on occasion, to be protected by a bodyguard. He spoke with remarkable clarity to the church's mission to the powerless within our society. In so doing he angered a significant portion of the Episcopal church, who were not willing to provide the supportive community that his ministry sought and needed. Yet Hines gave a credibility to the church's faith that few others were willing to risk.

There was no conversion in Hines' outlook. He came from a family of socially conscious people. He was born and reared in a small upland South Carolina town, Seneca, where his father was a physician. This is close to where William Porcher DuBose served his first church in Abbeville. Hines' mother was the Episcopalian and he followed her commitment. His Presbyterian father influenced both his strong social conscience — he brought the first black doctor to Seneca — and his gift of public speaking.

Hines went to college at the University of the South and to seminary at Virginia Theological Seminary. Because there were no openings in Upper South Carolina in the midst of the Depression, when he graduated from seminary in 1933, he went to the Diocese of Missouri, where the Bishop was William Scarlett (1883-1973). Scarlett was one of the controversial, prophetic figures of our church, who Hines greatly admired. Hines served in St. Louis at St. Michael's and All Angels Church under Karl Block (1886-1958), who later became Bishop of California. Block was a great preacher. Hines' beginnings in the ordained ministry were, therefore, entirely consistent with the bent of his mind from his youth.

After serving parishes in Augusta, Georgia, and Houston, Texas, he was elected Bishop Coadjutor of the Diocese of Texas in 1945. He became the Ordinary in 1955. During his time as Bishop of Texas, Hines was in the middle of the debate in the church concerning racial equality. He was clear and forceful on the issues, although it often appeared that he stood almost alone. The Diocese itself, as well as those institutions within it that Hines had worked to start and promote — school, hospital and seminary — suffered a financial loss because of the refusal of some of the people within the Diocese to rally around the witness of their Bishop. Needless to say, this was a source of pain for him, for he had nothing to gain by alienating members of his diocese; yet his priorities were, as they have always been, clear. Bishop Hines is a man of great pastoral concern, but he has never allowed this to cloud the church's need to speak out in the face of oppression and injustice.

In 1964 at St. Louis where he started his ordained ministry, John Hines was elected Presiding Bishop of the Episcopal Church. Right from the start he called the church to sacrifice in the cause of racial justice and the urban crisis. In August 1967, in the wake of the urban riots, he took a walking tour in Brooklyn and Detroit. Out of this the conviction was cemented that the Episcopal Church was called by God to do something extraordinary to empower the dispossessed. At the General Convention that year in Seattle, Hines asked the Episcopal church to:

> take its place, humbly and boldly, alongside of, and in support of, the dispossessed and oppressed people of this country for the healing of our national life.

He called for a program which came to be called the General Convention Special Program (GCSP), whose aims will be the bringing of people in the ghettos into areas of decision making by which their destiny is influenced. It will encourage those of political and economic power to support justice and self-determination for all men.

The Seattle General Convention passed the GCSP — the name given to it by the Executive Council several months later — and $3 million for each of the next three years was earmarked for its purposes. It immediately ran into controversy over the handling of grants. Undoubtedly mistakes were made, but Hines stood behind the principle and the storm mounted. In 1968, membership declined in the Episcopal church for the second year in a row and giving began to fall off. The House of Bishops meeting in 1968 reaffirmed conscientious objection to a particular war (i.e., the Vietnam War).

In 1969 a special General Convention was held at the University of Notre Dame for the purposes of continuing church renewal. In the previous spring James Foreman and Lucius Walker had presented the Episcopal Church, among other denominations, with a *Black Manifesto* demanding $500 million in reparations from all the churches, including $60 million from the Episcopal Church. This added to the GCSP and the Vietnam War made certain that Notre Dame would be a controversial convention. Hines' leadership was unclouded. He believed the Episcopal church had to be responsive to the suffering in our society from whatever quarter it came and the Convention generally supported him. The church, in the meanwhile, was becoming increasingly polarized.

In the 1970 General Convention at Houston, the GCSP was again the great issue. Some modifications in the program were worked out and Hines fought to keep the substance of the church's ministry to the oppressed from being destroyed. The convention voted to continue the GCSP for the next three years and the House of Bishops gave the Presiding Bishop a somewhat qualified vote of confidence. That following winter declining national revenues required that the personnel of the Executive Council be cut from 204 to 110 — a day that will long be remembered at 815 Second Avenue.

Between 1970 and 1973, the GCSP lost much of its vitality as the resistance to it in the church continued to grow. Hines continued to believe in it, but the spirit of the times was against him. While the Presiding Bishop was much admired for his courage, it seemed clear that the church was battle weary. The country was losing its nerve. The issues of the ordination of women to the priesthood and prayer book revision could wait no longer and we had only a certain amount of energy. Having decided to resign at the Louisville General Convention in 1973, Bishop Hines' address there called for the church not to retreat from this mission. "What is at stake," he said, "is not just the future of a program (GCSP) but the integrity of the Church's life and the credibility of our witness to Christ as Lord of all."

The church did retreat. The previous six years had been heady times and there was a kind of excitement and urgency to our life. The next six years brought conflict and strong feelings as we hammered out the inhouse questions of prayer book and women's ordination. Yet, somehow, we suspected that, as John Hines sometimes in good humor suggested, we were "rearranging the deck chairs on the Titantic," if we did not return to the prophetic witness of the church. What did not vanish was the quiet, faithful and challenging witness of Bishop Hines. He remains an effective sign of one of our more courageous moments as a church and of an unfinished task before us.

The Episcopal church, as any Christian body, must ask itself what happens when the Gospel is truly preached. What do we expect our hearing to effect in our action? At least three possible answers come to mind.

First, we can begin longing for heaven. Edward Bouverie Pusey (1800-1882), the wealthy Tractarian, preaching in the poor house in England comes to mind. We have his sermons preached there in published form. It is incredible to think the poor understood them and for that we can be thankful. What he tells them is that it is fortunate they suffer now, because this will assure them a better place in heaven. The Episcopal plantation owners in the South, incidently, were telling their slaves essentially the same thing.

I call this, after the black spiritual, the "Old Black Joe" syndrome. Karl Marx called it the opiate of the people. It reminds us of the belief in ancient times, when people practiced animal sacrifice, that the gods liked the internal organs and not the steaks and chops. Consequently, the intestines and such were consumed by the sacrificial fire for the gods to eat and the steaks and chops were given to the priests and their families. It is a very convenient division, which enables us to live in comfort now in the assurance that it will all work out in heaven. Of course, this requires for its validity a very literal notion of heaven, as well as a certain gullibility about our own motivations.

Secondly, we can expect the Gospel to justify the righteous on earth. It is remarkable that we can read the New Testament and Jesus' condemnation of the Pharisees and still believe this, but the powers of self-justification in religious people have always been amazing. Sometimes it can have a reverse twist to it. There is the delightful story of the priest preaching on the parable of the Pharisee and tax-gatherer, both of whom went to the temple to pray (Luke 18:9-14). As the story goes, the Pharisee thanks God that he is not as the tax-gatherer, a sinner, and then recounts all the righteous things he has done. The tax-gatherer simply asks God to have mercy on him, a sinner. The question Jesus raised was which man went from the temple justified. The preacher at this point was reported to have said, "O Lord, we thank you that we are not as this Pharisee," implying that like the tax-gatherer we are justified by boasting in our confession of sin.

The claim that our way of life is God's intention for all people is the presupposition that lies behind all movements that imply God is on our side. The idea that God loves America and hates the Soviet Union is only the most crass form of persistent temptation to think that a given ideology, economic system, set of values or point of view has God's particular blessing. The belief is that God legitimates or sanctifies our own self-interest.

Both of these responses to the question of what we expect the Gospel to effect among us when it is truly heard draw on a static picture of the world. Neither require any change now. The first response postpones the resolution of why some people must suffer. The second response either ignores the issue or implies people suffer because they do not have faith. Certainly this follows from the words of someone like Robert Schuller of the "crystal cathedral" in Los Angeles, who resolves everything by saccharine preaching of something called "possibility thinking." Possibility thinking implies that whatever you wish which accords with prevailing values can be yours by thinking rightly.

A third response to the expected effect of the Gospel is not uniquely Anglican, but is a reasonable result of reading the Scriptures in the light of history, which is an Anglican way of responding. It is that we all change now and forever and the issue is how shall we change. We are that to which we relate, and the Christian changes by relating to Christ. We are transformed by acquiring the mind of Christ. We can expect in that transformation to be judged; we can also hope to be made whole. It is part of a process to which we committed ourselves in baptism, and the one sure thing is that nothing will remain the same. For this we are profoundly grateful, for this is far from a perfect world and it is good news that creation is as yet unfinished.

Part of this understanding requires that we see our lives as interconnected. This is fundamentally Anglican. Our spirit, mind, emotions and body are inseparably united, as are our personal, interpersonal, historic, social and cosmic lives. We cannot postpone the issue of justice to a future date; we cannot ignore the hungry at our doorstep; and we cannot pretend that what we do in our business has no effect upon the state of our soul. There is a continuity to human existence, including between nature and supernature, which God confronts and, we pray, makes whole. The wholeness requires a church that is faithful to her Lord. We cannot "get off the hook" by disclaiming responsibility or postponing it to a future time.

It is possible for the Christian to refuse to see the implications of Christ for his or her manner of living. It is a blasphemy to suggest that this is a matter of indifference and the prophet who challenges him is meddling in what is none of his or her business. There is nothing outside God's business. If what the prophet says is not of God, ultimately that is the prophet's problem. God will not be without his witnesses. God speaks and we as Christians must discern what he says to us now, in this place. Such discernment requires an ability to think with the left hand — i.e., to be imaginative. The fact that it may make us uncomfortable is not the issue. The question is whether or not we hear and act. For that we all shall have to answer.

Ultimately the authenticity of faith and belief is measured at the bar of justice. All religious questions merge into the one query: What shall we do? There is an inevitable course to our religious profession, which can be aborted only by denying its Lord. That course leads to living in the world as God sees the world. We can debate the trivial points, but the vision is largely clear. To love God is to relieve the burden of all who suffer. The rest is a question of tactics.